D0875465

WRITING
THE NEWS

WRITING
THE NEWS

PRINT JOURNALISM IN THE ELECTRONIC AGE

by WALTER FOX

COMMUNICATION ARTS BOOKS

HASTINGS HOUSE, PUBLISHERS
New York 10016

ST. PHILIPS COLLEGE LIBRARY

808.066

F794

Copyright (c) 1977 by Walter J. Fox, Jr.

All rights reserved. No part of this publication may be reproduced, stored in a retrieval system, or transmitted, in any form or by any means, electronic, mechanical, photocopying, recording or otherwise, without the prior permission of the copyright owner or the publishers.

Library of Congress Cataloging in Publication Data

Fox, Walter.
    Writing the news.
    (Communication arts books)
    Includes index.
    1. Journalism—Authorship.   I. Title.
PN4783.F64   808′.066   77-562
ISBN 0-8038-8081-2
ISBN 0-8038-8082-0 pbk.

Published simultaneously in Canada by
Saunders of Toronto, Ltd., Don Mills, Ontario

Printed in the United States of America

CONTENTS

59158

PREFACE

From the time that electronic media entered the province of journalism, the prevailing mood among newspapermen has been one of fear mingled with nostalgia.

The fear has been expressed in many ways: as outright attempts to obstruct the progress of the new media, such as the publishers' embargo on wire service news to radio stations in 1933; later, as militant optimism about the future of newspapers—a cheerleader's stance that coupled survival with hard work and the will to win—and, among reporters, as a secret dread that somehow they were the last remnants of a dying species.

Nostalgia—the attitude that the best days of print journalism were past—was easy to come by in the off-duty conversations of working newspapermen. But it was also implied in many journalism textbooks that looked back with pride to the days of the great reporters and the powerful dailies.

Both emotions are understandable in view of the early havoc wreaked by electronic media on print journalism and its institutions, and as a response to the vivid new dimensions given to reporting by radio and television. What is surprising, however, is that six decades into the electronic age, so many newspapermen and journalism texts still harbor these feelings.

The brilliant investigative reporting that uncovered the Watergate scandals of the Nixon Administration unquestionably has served to restore confidence in the latent power of print media. Yet, since the focus of these revelations has been the daily press, much of the publicity surrounding them, including the gripping film version, may have the ultimate effect of obscuring many subtle but profound changes in the role of print media that have been brought about by electronic pressure.

It should be obvious by now that neither despair nor mindless optimism are adequate responses to the challenge of a new age. There is ample evidence—especially in the emergence since television of whole new categories of print media—to suggest that the newspaper and magazine forms may be entering a new and vital period of community service, despite a somewhat lower profile in the coverage of national affairs and, locally, in spot news reporting.

It is the purpose of this book, therefore, not only to teach the fundamentals of news writing in a period of transition for print journalism, but also to point out how these techniques have been modified by the new electronic environment and to provide a rough outline of the context in which they are likely to be applied.

If, in the early chapters, the author takes a long look backward, it is not out of nostalgia, but only to show how the craft of news writing has evolved to its present state. Implicit in the book is the assumption that the evolutionary process continues unabated and that the student will play a key role in carrying it further.

Rules for the preparation of copy have not been included in this book because it is the author's belief that they are more effectively taught by the individual instructor who can adapt them to his own specific requirements. And since excellent guides to newspaper style, covering capitalization, abbreviations, punctuation, etc., are readily available from the Associated Press and United Press International, none has been included.

Finally, the author takes this opportunity to thank everyone who has assisted him in the preparation of this book, but—most of all—his wife, Francine, whose unfailing support and encouragement has made its publication a reality. To her it is dedicated with love.

Walter Fox

Philadelphia
February, 1977

1 : THE NEWSPAPER AS AN ART FORM

If the theories of Marshall McLuhan have stirred up a hornets' nest in traditional journalistic circles, they have also forced newspapermen as a whole to take a much harder look at their own medium. It is largely to the credit of this enigmatic Canadian seer that we have come to see the newspaper for what it really is: an art form.

When daily newspapers were the dominant news medium in the period that roughly paralleled the industrial expansion of the country, few editors would have made so exaggerated a claim for their own, often frenzied, efforts. And far too many journalists, whose early instruction in writing was received at the hands of literary-minded English teachers, suffered pangs of guilt in learning the style that newspapers demanded.

But looking back from the vantage point of the electronic age, and aided by the insights of McLuhan and other critics, we can observe much more clearly the peculiar characteristics of the newspaper medium. From this perspective, the newspaper appears as a corporate or collective form of the printed word, with a certain mosaic quality that allows for a considerable degree of participation by the reader. In his book *Understanding Media,* McLuhan describes this quality perceptively: "It is the daily communal exposure of multiple items in juxtaposition that gives the press its complex dimension of human interest."

The underlying "message" of the newspaper medium, apart from the content of stories, is to proclaim the existence of a community—geographic, political, ethnic or, as we saw in the

I

ST. PHILIPS COLLEGE LIBRARY

"underground" press of the late 1960s, generational. While not a "fine" art, in the strict sense of the term, the newspaper is nonetheless an art form and as "artful" in its own way as any of the corporate products of earlier periods.

Only when we are able to look at the newspaper this way—as a distinct medium and not a development or degeneration of the book or magazine forms—are we able to think realistically about it. Only then do the demands which the medium imposes on its writers seem as natural as the peculiar styles that the book and manuscript forms imposed on theirs.

By considering the newspaper as an art form we are also better able to trace its development during the last half of the 19th century and to understand the modifications it has undergone in this century as a result of electronic pressure.

The most dramatic evidence of this pressure can be seen in the general decline in numbers of daily newspapers in the United States from the peak of 2,200 in 1910 to 1,756 in 1975—one quarter of a century into the television era. In New York City alone, four major dailies closed during the 1960s.

As radio and then television took over many of the vital functions of the daily newspaper, specifically those related to the rapid movement of information, the old role of the daily newspaper as an exclusive channel of news changed abruptly. The ensuing years have been marked by the disappearance of newspapers that had taken on the quality of permanent institutions.

A parallel phenomenon is the highly visible struggle within the surviving dailies to find a role that is relevant to the electronic age. The cash prize contests that marked the panic period of the '50s have given way now to new emphasis on depth reporting and analysis, more dramatic use of photography, and experiments in make-up and graphic display. And there is no question that the investigative prowess displayed by several daily newspapers in unearthing the Watergate scandals of the Nixon Administration has helped to rejuvenate the medium.

But how successful any of this will be in arresting the general decline remains to be seen. What is important for the student of journalism to note is the profound impact electronic media have had on the daily newspaper, a product of 19th century technology.

Journalism educators, as a group, seem all too eager to overlook the nature of these effects, or to discount the evidence as a mere "updating" of what they believe is a basic journalistic form. What we are witnessing, however, may be a much more fundamental shift in the relative importance of media. If this is the case, to teach journalism with our eyes fixed on the daily newspaper would be a disservice to students who, more than most of us, are looking to the future.

When radio took from the daily newspaper its ability to get the news "first," the frantic era of "scoops" and "extras," characterized by the breathless reporter in a pork pie hat, ended once and for all. Newsmen whose chief assets were fleetness of foot or speed on a typewriter suddenly took on a comic aspect.

Even more comic—in retrospect—was the reaction of the newspaper industry to the new medium. Rather than adapt to changing media conditions, the newspaper publishers voted in 1933 to turn back the clock by cutting off news services to radio stations. As with most counter-revolutionary measures, the news blackout only served to speed up the revolution. Released from their dependency on the newspapers, radio networks began energetically to develop their own newsgathering expertise. The resulting systems not only thwarted the intent of the publishers' embargo, but also laid the groundwork for radio's brilliant coverage of World War II.

Newspapers had barely recovered from this first blow to their pre-eminence as a news medium when television delivered the knockout punch. Heralded as the ultimate entertainment medium, television quickly established itself in the news field, and in the process by-passed city rooms and editorial offices. Newspaper reporters covering the Army-McCarthy hearings in 1953 found themselves in the awkward position of writing for an audience that had witnessed the proceedings and was as familiar with the participants as it was with its own next-door neighbors.

We live today in the wake of an electronic revolution. Confusion and uncertainty abound, and while many persons—newspaper publishers included—prefer, in McLuhan's image, to go forward looking in the rear-view mirror, a few realities, however indistinct, are beginning to emerge.

One is that the daily newspaper is no longer the *prime* news medium. Television is, simply because it can take the viewer to the event; newspapers need middlemen. A corollary is that people don't need daily newspapers as much as they used to.

Another reality is that television is reshaping the perceptive powers of its audience and changing reader expectations of print media. As a result, traditional newspaper make-up seems anemic and dull. Advertising agencies understand this; many publishers still do not. And thus the striking contrast in most newspapers between display advertising and editorial layout. In some ways, the emergence of the underground press was as much a protest against visual blandness as it was against editorial rigidity.

Of most significance to prospective journalists, however, is that while daily newspapers have declined in importance, weekly news media are on the upsurge. Under the term "weekly" we can include national, regional and city-wide newspapers as well as small community publications. Even the older, well-established newsmagazines, *Time* and *Newsweek,* have undergone dramatic growth since the advent of television.

Too many journalists still fail to recognize that while electronic media gained an ever-increasing share of spot news coverage, they also released newspapers from the task of getting news "first" and offered them the opportunity of getting it "better." If the newsgathering functions of the newspaper were reduced in this process, the medium was given a new and more significant role as interpreter of the events that move so swiftly through the picture tube.

This new emphasis on "depth" and "interpretation" in

news writing has worked to modify the definition of news itself. Stories that offer no real insight into events now tend to be pushed aside in favor of more meaningful accounts. According to David B. Wilson, a columnist for the *Boston Globe,* a shift in news values was responsible for the closing of the press room at Boston Police Headquarters:

> What happened to the press room was that it became obsolete. The product that it produced, like the detachable collar and the buggy whip, no longer found a market.
>
> Liquor store holdups. Bookie raids. Two alarm fires. Automobile collisions. Storms, heat waves, floods. Abortion rings smashed. Lost children. Car chases. Burglaries. Gang wars. Shootings, knifings, beatings, killings. Life. Death.
>
> Such events are occasionally news even today. But this is true only if the protagonists are prominent, the offense or injury is extraordinarily grave or the act involves some other issue.
>
> The simple fact that someone has been robbed or deprived of light or heat or maimed by a motor vehicle or burned or shot to death is of insufficient interest to merit publication in a metropolitan newspaper. And it was precisely this kind of fact that the press room furnished its employing publisher and the general public.
>
> There is no shortage of such facts to report. They are not reported and published because editors and publishers have sensed that they no longer interest readers.

Once newspapers have been released from the instantaneous transmission of news, frequency of publication becomes less important. And if interpretation becomes a primary objective, then the perspective of a week is more advantageous than the 24-hour segment of the daily newspaper, or the encapsulated bulletins of the hourly newscast. The weekly *National Observer* has made this reality the basis of a profitable enterprise that would have been unthinkable before television.

Interpretation and spot news can be combined, and a growing number of daily newspapers are attempting to provide news-in-depth alongside spot news reporting, but it should be emphasized, nonetheless, that television, by converting a liability into an asset, has given the weekly newspaper a new and exceedingly vital function in society.

With the increased demand for more comprehensive coverage of community affairs, the role of even the small town weekly has taken on added importance. As the well-defined cities of 19th century America diffused under pressure of the motor car into today's urban "regions," daily newspapers found themselves hard put to provide adequate coverage of civic and political activities in the remote suburbs.

It was not at all unusual, in the critical period of suburban growth before and after World War II, for the average commuter to know more about governmental affairs in the city where he worked than he did about the elemental facts of political life in the township where he lived, paid taxes and educated his children. It was a situation made to order for corrupt politicians, and countless suburban communities still live with the consequences of venal administrators who were free to operate unchecked and unobserved.

One response by daily newspapers to the dissolution of the old city-community was to establish "zone sections." These were pages of local news inserted once or twice weekly in the regular edition and distributed within the appropriate zone. In many instances, zone sections were put together downtown by non-resident editors who depended on stringers and part-time correspondents for their knowledge of the area. It is not surprising, therefore, that the results tended to be superficial and lacking in any real grasp of political realities in the areas covered.

Yet, in a media situation that all but shouts for the emergence of vigorous, community-based weekly newspapers, relatively few publishers have responded. Most are content to meet 19th century expectations and serve as channels of social trivia, public relations, and civic and commercial "boosterism." The exceptions to this rule, while few in number, are significant because they suggest some of the possibilities open to print media in an era dominated by electronic communications. It is no coincidence that today's most enterprising and imaginative weekly publications were founded after the advent of television broadcasting.

On any list of interesting new weeklies would be the *Maine Times,* a statewide newspaper that has become a major force for environmental protection in the region; Boston's *Phoenix* and *Real Paper,* two successful urban weeklies that have evolved from the "underground;" the *Pacific Sun,* a revamped "old" weekly that offers incisive political coverage of suburban San Francisco, and the *Piedmont Virginian,* a new weekly covering a "community of interest" that spans several rural Virginia counties.

These newspapers serve an unusually diverse readership, ranging from Virginia farmers to Bay Area sophisticates, from Maine lobstermen to college-age Bostonians. And while each displays an authentic regional character, as a group they share certain fundamental similarities.

All place great emphasis on the intelligent coverage of local affairs, both in news and features, and are willing to explore in depth controversial local issues. To achieve this goal they will depart, on occasion, from the traditional news writing style of the daily newspaper.

All exhibit a genuine custodial interest in their own respective areas and regularly take editorial positions opposing projects which they feel to be harmful to the community—environmentally or politically—even when such projects are supported by local officials and organizations.

Finally, all of the above papers exploit the possibilities of modern printing technology—in typography, layout and photographic display—and provide readers with a product that is as visually attractive as it is editorially stimulating.

Among other new publications of interest to prospective journalists are the city and regional magazines that have risen to considerable prominence during the past decade in just about every major urban area. The best of these publications rely on investigative reporting and in-depth feature treatment of topics that, until recently, were ignored or superficially covered by daily newspapers. In one ironic case, a municipal scandal resulting in the conviction and imprisonment of a local daily newspaper reporter was uncovered by the city magazine.

What we are witnessing, in short, is the beginning of a new era of journalism, an era marked by the fragmenting of traditional information structures and the emergence of new and diverse forms of print media. For the person about to begin a career in journalism, this situation has practical implications.

It means that as a writer he will have to be extremely flexible. He must be able to write a vigorous "today" lead, but he must also be able to assess news developments from the perspective of a week or longer and write as compellingly of trends and patterns in the news as he does about a four-alarm fire.

It means that as an analyst he will have to probe well below the surface of events if he is to satisfy an audience increasingly concerned with information-in-depth. The words of the European statesman who admonished his aides, "Don't tell me what happened, tell me what it means!" have become a maxim for the contemporary journalist.

The changed media situation also implies that writers must be open to new ideas and new sources of information, even when these arise among small groups that may be objects of ridicule or contempt to the majority. Electronic technology makes information readily available to all segments of society, and any attempt to deal with social or political issues, especially from a journalistic perspective, must take this fact into account.

Finally, the failure of so-called "objective" journalists to provide any real understanding of the critical issues of the 1960s, suggests that newspapermen and women who hope to have some impact on the events which they are reporting will need to adopt a much less detached stance. Facing an array of catastrophic threats to human survival, the world is in desperate need of journalists who, in the words of Jack Newfield, "are committed in their bones, to not just describing the world, but changing it for the better.''

While it is beyond the province of this book to discuss the techniques of press photography, it should be emphasized, nevertheless, that the expanded use of this medium in communicating the news requires that newsmen today be as familiar with a camera as they are with a typewriter. Many smaller publications cannot justify the expense of a photographic department, and reporters are expected at least to take their own pictures, if not develop and print them.

In the chapters that follow we shall attempt to describe in detail those skills which will be useful to the journalist in a time of widespread change, both within his profession and in the world at large.

2 : THE STRUCTURE OF THE NEWS STORY

The modern news story has become so pervasive a form in American culture that its peculiar evolution during the past 200 years has gone by almost unnoticed, even by journalists.

College English classes still dissect the essays of Bacon and Addison and learn the rhyme scheme of the sonnet, but ask students to describe the characteristics of news writing and they will struggle to list more than a few adjectives. The form is so familiar that it is invisible.

Journalists, of course, are expected to master the art of news writing. But in doing so they tend to regard it as more or less of a fixed form, subject to innovation by the more gifted practitioners. They remain, nevertheless, generally unaware of the outside forces that have shaped and are constantly reshaping the news story.

What are these forces? Certainly, social convention and prevailing usage have played a part. And there is no question that the phenomenal expansion of literacy within the past century has significantly altered news writing by providing it with a mass audience. But far and away the most decisive factors in the evolution of news style have been the technological development of the newspaper itself and the interaction of the form with the new electronic media.

"If telegraph shortened the sentence," says McLuhan, "radio shortened the news story, and TV injected the interrogative mood into journalism." We might go further and suggest that the typewriter generated pressure for uncluttered prose and stylistic uniformity, and that the telephone, by making public figures readily accessible to newsmen, created a new journalistic staple—the direct quote.

By stressing the power of technology to shape the form of the news story, we do not thereby diminish either the skill or the creativity of the journalist. The effective communicator, in any age, is the one who is fully aware of the prevailing technologies and works within their framework to transmit his message. To point out that news writing is evolving in response to technological change is only another way of saying that it is a dynamic form of the written word—a form that remains in close touch with the mood and tempo of human affairs.

It is no coincidence that a major proportion of modern novelists, poets and playwrights have come from the ranks of newspaper reporters. Even the relatively few who bypassed this experience have been forced to adapt their style to the lean, verb-oriented prose that has come to characterize contemporary newspaper writing.

The long list of writers stretches from Mark Twain, who was associated in some way with newspapers for 18 years of his career, to John O'Hara, who was a reporter on newspapers in Pennsylvania and New York City before turning to fiction. It would also include Bret Harte, Stephen Crane, O. Henry, Theodore Dreiser, Sinclair Lewis, Sherwood Anderson, Ernest Hemingway, and John Hersey.

Both Walt Whitman and Carl Sandburg had considerable experience as newspapermen, and playwright Eugene O'Neill recalled that it was the publisher of the now-defunct New London *Telegraph,* where O'Neill served a brief and inauspicious stint as reporter, who first "really thought I had something to say, and believed I could say it."

NEWS WITHOUT STRUCTURE

One of the easiest ways to see how news style has evolved in the wake of technological change is to look at representative samples of the craft from its beginnings in the early 1700s to the present.

The Colonial newspaper, as it existed along the Eastern seaboard, was a primitive operation by modern standards. It was produced on a hand press with hand-set type by a printer who did job work on the side.

Rarely larger than four letter-sized pages and issued once or twice a week, the Colonial press served as a catch-all for news from the mother country (at least two months' old), correspondence purporting to explain political intrigue on the Continent, official proceedings of Colonial government and, in the relatively little space remaining, items of local interest.

The concept of reporting, as we understand it today, did not exist. Printers used whatever news came into their shop or what they could glean from other newspapers, foreign and domestic. The writing style varied from printer to printer, but it tended to be an artless, colloquial presentation. Since it was assumed that the reader eventually would read the entire paper, there was no need to structure stories to arouse interest.

Typical of Colonial news style is the following story from a July 1704 issue of the Boston *News-Letter,* the first regularly-published American newspaper:

> *Piscataqua, July, 6.* On Tuesday last eight Indians were seen at York, who had almost surpriz'd one *Shaw,* that was at some distance from the Garrison: The Indians were within Pistol Shot, and might have kill'd him, but striving still to surround & take him alive, (as supposed for Intelligence) he by that means, being a nimble active man, made his escape. Captain *Heath* & Lieutenant *March* immediately went in pursuit of them 6. or 7. Mils, but no discovery.

Although weekly newspapers multiplied along the Eastern seaboard during the early 1700s, the basic news style continued to be unstructured, informal and non-objective, as is evident in the following "crime" story from the Massachusetts *Spy* of 1770:

> *Portsmouth, September 14.* Last Wednesday was brought
> to town in irons, the notorious Cotterel and Badger, from Bos-
> ton, who were taken last Sunday night by the watchmen of
> that town, with large packs of goods and secured till the
> morning, when being carried before a magistrate, they con-
> fessed them to be the property of Mr. Joshua Wentworth of
> this town, whose store they broke open on the night following
> the 4th inst. and took goods to the amount of upwards of
> £4000. They charge one or two persons in town being con-
> cerned, and one is taken up, who denies knowing any thing of
> the affair. Badger is one who was concerned in setting fire to
> the new gaol in Boston, and last year was set on the gallows,
> but for the same: They are both old offenders, though young
> in years, and but little regard a whipping. It is now hoped they
> will meet with a punishment due to their crime. But a small
> part of the goods are yet got, they having hid them at different
> places on the road.

The first half of the 19th century saw considerable improve-
ment in printing technology. Most newspaper printers were
using iron presses which could produce a stronger and more
even impression over a larger area of type. This development
combined with new and more legible type faces made the newspaper of the day—usually four pages, tabloid size—a much
more attractive and readable product.

But even with these technological advances, the news story
continued to be rambling, obtuse and laced with moral indigna-
tion. It would not be until the late 1840s, with the introduction
of a new medium—the telegraph—that the news story would
begin a profound shift in structure.

TELEGRAPH NEWS

Every school child used to learn that on May 25, 1844,
Samuel F. B. Morse sat at a table in Washington and tapped out
the historic telegraph message, "What hath God wrought?" to
an assistant in Baltimore. Less widely known but far more important was what Mr. Morse did later that same day: he sent the

first telegraphic message published in a newspaper. Thus, within hours of the birth of the telegraphic medium, its marriage to the newspaper was consummated.

A more natural and fruitful union could hardly be imagined. Printing technology, by 1850, had undergone a quantum leap with cylinder presses harnessed to steam power. It was now possible to produce larger papers at an even faster rate. All that was needed was news to fill the growing space—and along came the telegraph!

It is interesting to note that, unlike radio, the telegraph never constituted a threat to newspapers, since its messages were in code and not readily available to the public. The telegraphic news bulletin had little value for anyone until it could be decoded, and it was the newspaper office that would become the decoding center for the man in the street.

As newspapers were linked to the telegraph wire, things began to happen to the news story. In the early days, telegraphic news appeared in bulletin form in a special column reserved for that purpose. Hence, at the outset, the telegraph made it necessary to boil down news stories to a summary of one or two sentences that eventually would become the "lead" or first paragraph of the modern news story. For more than three decades, the telegraphic bulletin and the older, more leisurely news style were juxtaposed on the same newspaper page. But whenever the telegraph key came into play, news writing was altered.

The changes in news writing set in motion by the telegraph were sped up considerably by the Civil War. Battlefield correspondents, who relied heavily on the telegraph for the transmission of dispatches, pruned their stories of opinion and excess description to reduce tolls. And there were other, unforseen problems.

After a major battle, it was not at all unusual for a half dozen or more correspondents to converge on a single telegraph operator, all demanding precedence on the wire. Simply to avoid bloodshed, harried telegraph operators devised a system whereby reporters would be permitted to send a paragraph of their story at a time. When each man had sent his first paragraph, the go-round would begin again with another paragraph. Thus, by constructing his story in an "inverted pyramid" style, with a general summary at the beginning and minor details at the end, the reporter was safe. Regardless of where it might be interrupted by a break in communications or a newspaper deadline, the story was a comprehensible whole.

Ultimately, telegraphic pressure would have similar effects within the newsroom. Linked to the telegraph network, a newspaper suddenly found it had more news than it could handle, and simply handling it became the specialized function of a new journalistic technician—the copy editor. With news moving at electric speed and its relative importance subject to instantaneous change, stories that could be constructed in a manner allowing for drastic cutting without rewriting made the task much easier. The inverted pyramid served this purpose admirably, by permitting news stories to be lopped from the bottom up as space requirements demanded.

In time, even the newspaper reader would benefit from the new telegraphic structure. As newspapers, aided by the technological advances in printing, expanded to accommodate the growing volume of telegraphic news and advertising, the reader was forced to pick and choose what stories he would read in their entirety. The inverted pyramid simplified this process by condensing the essential facts in the first paragraph.

The shift to the inverted pyramid as a model for all news, however, did not come about with any consistency until the end of the 19th century. It was delayed to some extent by the intentional policy of some publishers, notably Pulitzer and Hearst in New York and their imitators elsewhere, to single out sensational and human interest items and treat them in a style that would grip the reader's emotions. These stories, written in the manner of old-time pulp detective magazines, were rarely cut, while the more mundane news items were summarized in bulletin form in a separate column.

Another delaying factor at the local level was the ingrained habit of 19th century journalists to write news in a colloquial style. Such idiosyncrasies could be tolerated as long as newspapers were running 4- or 8-page editions. But when newspaper size doubled and tripled during the 1890s, a story structure that could be swiftly edited and cut would be demanded by copy desks.

In the 1880s, however, the Associated Press was instructing its writers to tell all of the important facts in the first paragraph, and it was an AP correspondent, John P. Dunning, covering the disastrous Samoan hurricane of 1889, who wrote what has become a classic lead of that era:

> Apia, Samoa, March 30.—The most violent and destructive hurricane ever known in the Southern Pacific passed over the Samoan Islands on the 16th and 17th of March, and as a result, a fleet of six warships and ten other vessels were ground to atoms on the coral reefs in the harbor, or thrown on the beach in front of the little city of Apia, and 142 officers and men of the American and German navies sleep forever under the reefs or lie buried in unmarked graves, thousands of miles from their native lands.

Although his lead would be considered excessively verbose by today's standards, Dunning had shown that a good writer could meet the demands of the telegraphic style and still convey the news in a dramatic and interesting manner. The Dunning story, and especially its lead, became a model of news style for young reporters in the 1890s.

TELEPHONE AND TYPEWRITER

By this time, two other new inventions, the telephone and the typewriter, had entered the newsroom, and each was having a profound impact on news writing. The telephone did for local news gathering what the telegraph had done for national coverage. Using the telephone, the city desk could direct the movements of its staff with maximum efficiency and receive immediate reports from newsmen at the scene of events.

But even more significant, as far as news writing is concerned, was the remarkable power of the telephone to penetrate the inner sanctums of social, economic and political life. Reporters found themselves talking on the telephone to public figures who previously had been inaccessible, and, without leaving the city room, could interview all of the principals in a news story. Now, major stories that lacked direct quotes would be bounced back by the copy desk to the derelict reporter.

There is probably no better example of the power of the telephone to command a response than a call placed by the Camden (N.J.) *Courier* on September 6, 1949, to Howard B. Unruh, a psychotic World War II veteran who had barricaded himself in his home after killing 13 persons in a mad rampage. Surrounded by police who were firing machine guns, shot guns and tear gas shells, Unruh picked up the phone and said, "Hello."

"Is this Howard?", an editor asked.

"Yes," Unruh replied.

"Why are you killing people?"

"I don't know. I can't answer that yet. I'll have to talk to you later. I'm too busy now."

If newspapers were at first cool to the blandishments of the typewriter, they warmed up considerably after 1884 when the Associated Press telegraph operators began using the contraption to produce clean and legible copy. After handling the neatly-typed stories from the wire service, it was not long before editors purchased the machines for their own writers. But the effects of the typewriter went far beyond cleaner and more readable copy.

The typewriter, as McLuhan has pointed out, "fuses composition and publication, causing an entirely new attitude to the written or printed word." By composing on the typewriter, the journalist becomes, in effect, his own publisher. As his ideas flow immediately into print, he becomes acutely aware of sentence structure, diction and the rhythm of words and phrases.

Forced by the typewriter to be both a writer and a critic of his own writing at the same time, the reporter soon discarded his verbose and colloquial style for the stripped-down prose that would become synonymous with newspaper journalism. It seemed almost as it the staccato movement of the machine had been transmitted to the writing it produced. Sentences gradually shortened and turned overwhelmingly to the active voice. Excess adjectives and adverbs were pruned to emphasize the verb. The "lead" took on a life of its own, with painstaking effort devoted to its construction.

But the new lean prose also pointed up sharply any stylistic vagaries among writers. To insure a uniform and homogenous product, publishers moved quickly to provide their staffs with guide books which settled arbitrarily all questions of capitalization, abbreviation and punctuation.

TELETYPE STYLE

If the telegraph had given the modern news story its basic structure, the typewriter generated its peculiar style. And it would be the combination of these two inventions in the teletype that provided the final impetus for standardization of the form among news writers.

After 1913, as the wire services gradually changed over from the telegraph key and Morse code to the teletype, the locus of news style became the central headquarters of the major press associations in New York. It was simply a matter of convenience. The teletype provided newspapers with complete, typed stories that merely had to be ripped from the machines, edited for capitalization—the teletype used only capital letters—or cut, if necessary. The sheer volume of wire copy made it far simpler for newspapers to adopt the style of the wire services than to make the wire copy conform to their own on a daily basis.

So it came about that in the first quarter of the 20th century, the press associations would assume responsibility for perfecting and polishing the news story. Since wire service stories would be relayed to all parts of the country, they had to be free of regional or idiomatic expressions. In the process of trying to strike a national mean, the wire services, as models, unintentionally created it.

A typical wire service story followed the inverted pyramid structure with a summary lead and an elaboration of the major aspects of the event in order of importance. The least important material was placed at the end where it could be cut without damaging the story. Wire service copy was tightly written and marked by smooth transitions from paragraph to paragraph and the positioning of key words at the beginning of sentences to heighten interest.

The following story, from the Associated Press in 1925, could serve as a classic example of the form at the peak of its development:

> NEW YORK, Feb. 5.—Praying, fasting and singing hymns, thirteen former Seventh Day Adventists on Long Island today are awaiting the end of the world.
>
> They think it will come tomorrow.
>
> They are led by Robert Reidt, who calls himself the "Apostle of Doom." The party includes men, women and children, and a family of four negroes.
>
> Most of them have sold their worldly goods, even part of their clothing, and are spending the last few days on carrots and water.
>
> Tomorrow they will go to a hill top near East Patchogue to hear the trumpet of doom. They expect to be taken in a cloud chariot to the woods near San Diego, Calif., where they say 144,000 "Brides of the Lamb" will be gathered.
>
> All other people will perish, according to their prediction.
>
> Announcement at headquarters of the Seventh Day Adventists at Washington that tomorrow is not the decreed date for the millennium has not affected the preparations of the little band.
>
> Mrs. Margaret W. Rowen, leader of those who have fixed the date for tomorrow, was denounced by the church leaders.
>
> It is the contention of the Adventist organization that the date fixed by her is extremely premature.

> The Seven Plagues—including the Great Battle of Armageddon—must come before the world's doom, it is maintained by the main group of Adventists.
>
> But Reidt has made his predictions in detail. The period of destruction, starting tomorrow midnight, will last for seven days, he says, with fire, disease, hailstones and pestilence striking the earth at one time.
>
> Reidt is himself no longer a member of the Adventist Church. He has sold his furniture to a secondhand dealer on condition he may buy it back.
>
> The Apostle of Doom—a pale faced, fat little man of thirty-three, with a buxom wife and four pallid, frightened-looking children between the ages of six and twelve, said he had seen a vision in which he had been shown how the messiah would appear to the faithful and transport them to San Diego.

The wire service story form was copied by reporters all over the country. If, at times, this was to the detriment of more original writing at the local level, it nevertheless provided a sleek and understated container for the news.

An even greater degree of dynamism was injected into wire service writing by the rivalry in the early 1920s between the older, more conservative Associated Press and the commercial upstart, United Press.

To enhance its competitive position against the AP, a member-owned cooperative whose copy tended to be sober and factual, the UP stressed colorful writing by its reporters. United Press editors supplied background to the news and sought out interviews, features and human interest items ignored by the AP. The strategy worked well. Impressed by the vivid, personal style of UP correspondents, many longtime AP members purchased the UP service as a second wire.

The UP's policy of hiring young men without experience gave it a reputation as a training ground for writers and reporters and further served to spread the wire service gospel. Men who had mastered the UP's crisp style, and who did not elect to remain with the service, found easy access to the city rooms of the major daily newspapers, where UP copy was held in high regard.

Looking back over the development of the news story, it would be fair to say that the form which had taken shape by the 1920s, with an assist from the wire services, was pre-eminently a product of 19th century technology. It had been shaped and abetted by every major invention of the industrial revolution, as was its matrix, the daily newspaper. With the exception of the teletype, which appeared in 1913, and the wirephoto, in 1935, the modern newspaper was complete in its essentials by the last decade of the 19th century.

Daily newspapers of this time had installed banks of Linotype machines, permitting operators to set type swiftly from a keyboard, and were printing on electrically-powered rotary presses capable of turning out 100,000 copies of a 12-page edition every hour. Newspaper layout utilized multicolumn headlines, line cuts and, thanks to the invention of the half-tone process in 1878, photographs. In the newsroom, typewriters clacked, telephones rang and telegraph keys stuttered in Morse code.

But in that same decade, as the elements of the modern newspaper coalesced, a young Italian physicist named Guglielmo Marconi was experimenting with a device for transmitting electromagnetic signals through the ether. The success of his invention, culminating in the development of radio, ushered in a new and far more disconcerting era for newspapers. For— unlike the telegraph—radio required no decoding process, and, as a carrier of news, would eventually by-pass print media.

THE ELECTRONIC REVOLUTION

The electric and mechanical technology of the 19th century had strengthened the position of the daily newspaper. It became increasingly clear, as the 20th century wore on, that electronic technology was challenging the old communication structures with wholly new media of its own: first radio, then the newsreel and documentary film, and finally television.

In the first chapter we noted the effects of this new technology on existing daily newspapers. Our concern at this point, however, is to assess the impact of the electronic revolution on the craft of news writing.

The first significant new departure in print journalism in the 20th century was the establishment of tabloid newspapers in the 1920s. While there is no evidence to suggest that its originators intended it as a direct response to radio, the tabloid form appears, in retrospect, to be an excellent adaptation to the changing media situation of that period. With radio moving into spot news coverage, including on-the-scene reports and interviews, the only real option for print media was to handle less news better. And this is what many tabloids did, despite the sensational nature of the material on which they focused.

With five columns of type on a vertical rectangle half the size of a standard newspaper page, the tabloid was ideally suited to the close coordination of photographs and type in magazine style. It enabled editors to single out certain stories and treat them in depth—both in words and pictures—and to condense and summarize the remaining news. It developed the news-feature, a story form that combined hard news with the techniques of fiction for maximum impact. Even in its condensation of straight news, the tabloid excelled in vivid writing that would be copied by the standard-sized dailies.

The New York *Daily News,* which began the tabloid era in 1919, remains the archetype of the form. Five years after it was started by Joseph Medill Patterson, the *News* reached a circulation of 750,000—the largest in the country. In 1947 it set an all-time circulation record of 2,400,000 daily and 4,500,000 Sunday. Although it has suffered losses in the wake of television, the *News* continues to maintain its number one position with a daily circulation in excess of 2,000,000.

As a daily newspaper format, the tabloid worked well in urban areas like New York where there were large numbers of commuters. It could be sold effectively on newsstands and read easily on subways and street cars. The form was not as adaptable to areas where home delivery by carriers constituted a major portion of circulation—it could not be folded into a throwable package. Only in recent years has the tabloid style fully come into its own as an increasingly popular format for weekly newspapers.

Another major innovation in print journalism during the "radio age" was the appearance of the weekly newsmagazines—first *Time* in 1923, then *Newsweek* a decade later, and finally *U. S. News & World Report*. Like the tabloid, the newsmagazine worked well in the new media situation created by radio. Aimed at what it described as the "busy" reader, the newsmagazine offered the major foreign and national news in well-written and entertaining summaries.

In its writing style, the newsmagazines went even further than the tabloids in departing from the standard news story structure. To give zest to news that often was a week old and already known in its essentials to readers, the newsmagazines turned back to the old narrative form, but in a smooth and sophisticated manner, and with a strong undercurrent of human interest. *Time*'s stated intention of making all of its copy appear to be written by one man, was eminently achieved, to the ensuing disdain of its critics who dubbed the inverted sentence structure and telescoped modifiers *"Time* style."

In stories, the newsmagazines—notably *Time* and to a lesser extent *Newsweek* and *U. S. News*—also blurred the traditional line between straight news and editorial comment. *Time* readily acknowledged that it was not "impartial," but argued that it was "fair" in not twisting the facts to support its views. Many journalists felt, however, that by providing ready-made opinions, *Time* had gone too far in packaging news for the "busy" reader. But the formula continues to be effective, as *Time*'s 4,000,000 circulation can testify.

Outside of the three major publications, newsmagazine style had little effect on news writing. A much less stylized version of the narrative form could be seen in the growing number of Sunday newspaper sections which reviewed the week's news. Nevertheless, it was becoming more and more evident that readers who had heard the Hindenburg zeppelin disaster by radio live from Lakehurst, N. J., and who had listened to Edward R. Murrow's broadcasts during the bombing of London in World War II, would come to expect more from print media than a standardized news story.

Even more fundamental than the emergence of radio as an important news vehicle was the fact that the new medium had created a seamless web of instantaneous communication covering the entire planet. By virtue of this fact, all news had a global dimension. It was no longer adequate for reporters simply to furnish a factual account of *what* had happened; of the traditional "five Ws" of reporting, the "Why" suddenly became paramount. In the electronic age, news needed meaning and context, and providing these took on a special name: interpretation.

Radio moved quickly to supply news analysis, and, despite the inherent limitations of its broadcast format for in-depth reporting, produced an array of "commentators" who combined a compelling oral delivery with perceptive insights on current events. Newspapers, still mesmerized by the old notion of "objectivity," were reluctant to take the plunge, even though the medium of print was ideal for the interpretative role.

Editors who had been trained in pre-radio journalism resisted the new movement to "interpretation" almost as much as they resisted the new medium itself. And for a time, the general unwillingness of the daily press to adapt to the new media situation allowed the newsmagazines and journals of opinion, among the print media, to monopolize news analysis by default.

The complex events leading up to World War II, including the civil war in Spain, put enormous pressure on daily newspapers to provide some explanation for the chaotic events in Europe. Accordingly, foreign correspondents were given a free hand to incorporate their own observations and judgments into their stories. But back home, a reporter covering city hall under the watchful eye of an old-school editor, had to bootleg such information under the guise of "informed sources."

Not until the 1950s, with the daily press scrambling for survival in the wake of television, did newspapers begin to experiment with a more meaningful presentation of the news. It would be another full decade, however, until the surviving dailies, goaded by the revelations of the "underground" press and the muckraking magazines, would fully embrace interpretation as a matter of policy.

The rest of the story is current history. Electronic technology has ushered in a new era of print journalism marked by a great diversity of style and structure, as well as by the flowering of new journalistic forms. No longer is the word "journalism" synonymous with the daily press, as it was in the 1920s. Within print media today, "journalism" includes local and national weeklies, newsmagazines, specialized news services, city and regional magazines, racial, ethnic and tribal newspapers, and independent publications serving vocational and professional groups.

Some of the most incisive political reporting and writing during the past decade has appeared in the *Village Voice* and *Rolling Stone,* two publications once closely identified with the counterculture.

Yet the present is built on the past. The great legacy of the age of the daily newspaper has been the development of a clear prose style, free not only of idiom and colloquialism, but also of the literary and moral cant that marred so much of 19th century writing.

The language of journalism is a kind of tempered English, a vigorous, disciplined prose forged in the industrial revolution and hardened in five decades of international conflict. It remains, even today, the most flexible and adaptable form of English and one which, in a new age, may just as effectively serve the cause of peace and human brotherhood. It is this language— style and structure—that we are about to study.

3 : THE IMPORTANCE
OF THE LEAD

We have seen in the preceding chapter how the telegraph revamped the news story, placing extreme emphasis on the first paragraph or "lead." In the early days of the telegraph style, the lead was expected to be a complete summary of the story, with enough details to stand alone if a deadline made it necessary.

Even a cursory examination of contemporary newspapers will indicate how far lead writing style has evolved since the 19th century. But one fact remains as true today as it was then: constructing a good lead is the news writer's most important task.

The question naturally arises, "What is a good lead?" The answer, of course will vary in its specifics, depending on the type of story being written. Nevertheless, there is a fundamental rule that can be applied to all lead writing, and it is this: an effective lead is one that will catch the reader's attention *honestly* and direct it to what the writer feels is the essential point or news angle of the story.

The art of lead writing, thus, has two distinct phases. The first is the process of distilling from the mass of facts, figures and quotations a single coherent statement which, in the writer's view, best expresses the meaning of the story. The second phase is the writing of this statement in a way that will give it maximum impact on the reader.

Since a large part of the first phase consists of value judgments made by the writer on the facts, it does not lie entirely within the province of journalism. It is affected to a consider-

26

able degree by the writer's maturity and his experience, both as a reporter and a human being. It is also relative to the context of the story and the readership for which it is intended.

For all of these reasons, the ability to extract lead statements is not a skill that is easily learned or taught in school. It is best acquired working for a newspaper or, at least, in a situation that closely approximates actual newspaper reporting. Writing the lead, however, is a purely journalistic function, and, while a writer may spend a lifetime trying out new devices, there are a few basic rules which, once mastered, can be used with maximum effect even by beginners.

For the sake of order, we shall divide our study of lead writing into two parts, structure and language.

THE STRUCTURE OF THE LEAD

Nowhere can the effect of electronic media on the news story be seen as easily as in the structure of the lead paragraph. In the heyday of the telegraphic style, from the late 1880s to the 1920s, the lead paragraph was a story in miniature, often consisting of two or three fact-filled sentences. The following example, taken from the *New York Times* of Feb. 4, 1895, is fairly typical of the period:

> CHICAGO, Feb. 3.—Great excitement prevailed for hours this afternoon and evening among the people along the shore of Lake Michigan, from South Chicago to Whiting, Ind., on account of a general circulation of the report that the hull of the steamer Chicora, which was lost on Jan. 21 or Jan. 22, was floating outside the ice fields between those places, and that the forms of human beings could be discerned moving on the hull.

If the above example seems almost comical by contemporary standards, we must realize that leads were written that way not out of ignorance or a lack of sophistication, but simply because they had to be. All news flowed through the telegraph wire, and for a major story to overcome the numerous obstacles to transmission, not to mention newspaper deadlines, the story had to be constructed in self-contained units. Even if no further information were received by the newspaper, the lead could stand by itself as a front-page bulletin.

With the arrival of radio in the 1920s as an alternative news medium, the pressure on the telegraph newspaper began to ease, and while leads continued to be long—almost always two sentences—there was a perceptible decline in the number of facts included. Lead writing, at this time, began the gradual movement towards the uncluttered contemporary style.

Such a shift is evident by 1926, as this example from the Philadelphia *Public Ledger* of May 1 indicates:

> Samuel Holt, paymaster of Armour & Co., was slain by payroll bandits yesterday afternoon at 11th and Noble Sts. Caught between a crossfire of lead, he slumped to the floor of his automobile, riddled with bullets.

Radio had broken the absolute domination of the "five Ws"—who, what, when, where, and why. Readers who had heard a news bulletin on the radio were not interested in a simple repetition of the facts; they wanted an explanation. Thus, it was pressure from radio that raised to new prominence the often neglected "how" in newspaper lead writing. The movement to simpler lead forms, begun under pressure from radio, was accelerated by the increased use of photographs in newspapers. One good photograph of a five-alarm fire made adjectives superfluous.

As radio moved strongly into news coverage during World War II, newsmen became more selective in composing leads, using only those "Ws" which they felt were really necessary to the story. The others would be held for later paragraphs.

After the war, the wire services, which were becoming more and more aware of the shift in story values, hired "readability experts" to study their copy and make recommendations. One of these experts, Dr. Rudolph Flesch, had developed a "formula" for measuring readability. The most readable writing, according to the Flesch formula, is made up of words averaging 1.5 syllables and sentences averaging no more than 19 words. Acting on this advice, the Associated Press succeeded in reducing its average lead sentence length from 27 to 23 words and its word length in leads from 1.74 to 1.55 syllables.

Another expert, Robert Gunning, who was retained by the United Press, had reached similar conclusions and developed what he called a "Fog Index" to measure the complexity of writing. By applying the Gunning index, the UP simplified its writing style so that it would be understood by readers with 11.7 years of education. The wire service formerly had been writing at a level suitable for readers with 16.7 years of education, according to Gunning.

As might be expected, the attempt to apply a scientific yardstick to a craft as imprecise and volatile as news writing drew sharp criticism from many journalists who felt that the various formulas were, in effect, a literary strait jacket. But the wire services, as we have noted, were able to make their own writers conform at least to the general recommendations of the experts, and the simplified copy flowing from teletypes in hundreds of city rooms across the country ultimately would have its impact on newspaper style.

If the experts failed in the long run, to obtain a universal acceptance of their formulas, they did succeed in forcing journalists to look much more closely at their own writing in terms of clarity and readability. In this process, newspaper style was improved.

The combined pressure of radio and the formulas of the readability experts had produced a lead that by the end of the 1950s consisted of a single sentence, usually less than 25 words in length, which played up only the most important elements of the story. The following example, from the Philadelphia *Evening Bulletin* of Feb. 24, 1954, is typical of the crisp new lead style that would prevail in daily newspapers right up to the present:

> The much-debated charter amendments today appeared headed for a floor fight in City Council.

Today, when we talk about writing leads, we mean the ability to construct a single emphatic sentence that conveys the essential news elements of a given story.

Obviously, a story is selected because of its interest or importance to a large number of readers. Which news elements are "essential" in the lead and which are not will depend to some degree on several factors, among them the nature of the publication, whether it is issued daily or weekly, geographic and regional considerations, and, ultimately, the readership to which it is directed.

In certain categories of news stories, such as accidents, fires and disasters, there is a long-standing consensus among newspapermen that death and injury to victims must be spelled out in the lead. In stories of sporting events, final scores should appear in the lead. Beyond these special kinds of stories, however, the decision as to what must be included is made by the writer within the context of his publication.

Our concern in this chapter is not so much what must be included as, having decided what to include, how to express it as emphatically as possible in one sentence. And it is at this point that our instruction sharply veers away from English composition as it is traditionally taught.

Unlike the first sentence of most English themes, the lead of a news story is *not* a preface. It does not lead up to the story or prepare the reader for what is to come. In a news story, the lead is the story—in a nutshell!

Constructing an effective lead, therefore, requires the writer to confront the whole story at the outset in some meaningful way. For most beginners in news writing, this is the greatest obstacle they will have to overcome, since it stands in direct opposition to writing habits acquired over the years in English classes. It is a technique that must be mastered, however, since it is a fundamental skill of journalism.

Aside from its role in conveying the essence of a news story, the lead also determines to a large extent the shape and tone of the material that will follow. So organic is this relationship that it is difficult, if not impossible, to write a good story under a poorly-constructed lead. Thus, the inordinate amount of time and effort which most journalists put into lead writing pays off later in the form of a smoothly-running story.

THE LANGUAGE OF THE LEAD

In our definition of the lead, we described it not simply as a sentence, but as an *emphatic* sentence. This means that the lead must be constructed in such a way as to obtain maximum impact for the ideas expressed.

To achieve impact, the journalist draws upon all of the traditional emphatic devices of the English language, but some he adapts to his own purposes. In lead writing, the most useful techniques for gaining emphasis are word order, voice, verb selection and subordination.

Word Order

In English composition classes, students learn that the most emphatic parts of a sentence are the beginning and the end. But since climactic order normally is stressed, the end takes precedence as the most emphatic position.

On a newspaper page, however, every story is in direct competition with every other story for the reader's attention, and to hold back key information until the end of the lead might lose potential readers of the story.

At least that is the theory. Whether it really happens or not is a moot question. Writers have been constructing leads on the basis of this theory for so long that newspaper readers are trained to expect the most important element to appear at the beginning.

Thus, for lead writing, the old composition dictum is reversed: the beginning of the sentence is the most emphatic, and the end, next in emphasis. The middle, as always, is reserved for material to be de-emphasized.

Regardless of theory, the rule fits the general thrust of news writing practice, that is, order of importance—whatever is most important goes first.

Here is an emphatic lead from United Press International:

> NEW YORK—A horse-to-horse chase right out of the wild west last night led to the arrest in Times Square of a man on suspicion of driving a four-horse stagecoach while drunk.

If we attempt to rearrange the elements of this lead according to climactic order, as in the following example, the decline in emphasis becomes immediately apparent:

> NEW YORK—A man was arrested in Times Square last night on suspicion of driving a four-horse stagecoach while drunk, after a horse-to-horse chase right out of the wild west.

This awareness may be simply the result of our own lifelong conditioning as newspaper readers, but it is nonetheless true. If we wish to produce an emphatic news lead we must keep the important elements in the beginning of the sentence.

A corollary of this rule is that we avoid cluttering the opening of our lead sentence with unimportant or meaningless words or phrases. Strong leads usually begin with names or nouns, rarely with prepositions and participles. Articles can be dropped when they do not aid meaning. Useless phrases, such as ''The fact that . . .'' or ''For the purpose of . . .'' should always be eliminated, even if it means rewriting the sentence.

Voice

Since the active voice of verbs is ordinarily stronger and more emphatic than the passive, it is preferred for news writing, especially in the construction of leads.

It is much more emphatic to write:

> A car that ran out of control on Main st. early today damaged three parked vehicles before coming to rest in the window of a dress shop near 17th st.

Than to use the passive voice:

> Three parked vehicles and a storefront were damaged early today by a car that ran out of control on Main st. near 17th.

Having made this general rule, we must proceed to qualify it by pointing out that in many instances the passive is the more natural and emphatic form. When the receiver of the action is more significant than the doer, the use of the passive voice permits us to put that element at the beginning of the sentence, which, as we have already noted, is the most emphatic position.

Here is a front-page lead from the *New York Times:*

> BEIRUT, Lebanon, July 12—Col. Ernest R. Morgan of the United States Army, who was kidnapped by leftists 13 days ago, was released unharmed this evening to Premier Rashid Karami of Lebanon.

The writer in this example has correctly used the passive voice to emphasize Col. Morgan, whose fate had been the primary concern of American readers for almost two weeks.

After some experience in writing leads, the beginning journalist will find that the choice between active and passive verb forms becomes almost subconscious, determined largely by what element of the lead he wishes to emphasize.

A more common problem, even among experienced newsmen, is a tendency to use passive verb forms rather than a single, active verb. Unless the writer keeps a critical eye on his own prose, he is likely to slip into a lead like this:

> After months of unsuccessful attempts to sell a controversial tax package to Greensburg residents, City Manager Frank Gibson tendered his resignation today to City Council.

It would be more emphatic in this instance to move the news angle to the front of the sentence and to simplify the verb:

> City Manager Frank Gibson resigned today after months
> of unsuccessful attempts to sell a controversial tax package to
> Greensburg residents.

All vague and passive verb forms, such as "gave consideration to," "took into custody," or "was the recipient of," should be discarded in favor of the single, active verb. All of which brings us to our next point.

Verb Selection

If there is one element that distinguishes a living sentence from a static group of words, it is a strong verb. No adjective, however carefully chosen, can make up for the loss of emphasis caused by a weak or poorly-chosen verb.

The reason for this lies in the nature of language itself. In any sentence, the verb is responsible for galvanizing all of the other parts into coherent movement. By selecting verbs that are vigorous and descriptive, we provide, in effect, the highest possible voltage for the sentence and maximum impact for the ideas which it conveys.

News writing practice, with an eye to space limitations, has always stressed the importance of strong verbs, especially in leads. But even if space were not an issue, the key to vigorous writing lies in the careful selection of verbs.

In the following example, the writer attempts to describe a fire by using an adjective:

> The raging fire, fanned by heavy winds, was out of control for more than five hours.

The intended effect, however, is quickly dissipated by the use of a form of the verb "to be," the weakest possible verb in the language. By simply moving the description into the verb, we can obtain the impact that the writer intended:

> The fire, fanned by heavy winds, raged out of control for more than five hours.

What we are looking for, in short, are verbs that tell us not only *what* happened, but also *how* it happened.

It might be perfectly adequate to say, "The prosecution's star witness entered the courtroom." Adequate, that is, for the court record, but not adequate for a news story if, in fact, the witness had a broken ankle. In which case the reporter should write, "The prosecution's star witness limped into the courtroom."

In lead writing, where we are seeking maximum impact with a minimum of words, we would say that traffic "choked" rather than "filled" the downtown area, that hail storms "ravaged" rather than "destroyed" crops, or that striking bus drivers "shouted down" rather than "rejected" a proposed settlement. In each case we are selecting a verb that arouses some sensory response in the reader.

To obtain this effect, however, we cannot go beyond the facts of the story. Use of the verb "shouted down" implies that an emotional voice vote was taken by the strikers. The verb "ravaged" suggests violence and unusually heavy damage. In our search for the telling verb, accuracy remains the final criterion.

Subordination

The term "subordination," as applied to writing leads, means simply that the writer take pains to avoid frustrating the natural emphatic hierarchy of sentence structure.

Or to put it another way: the writer must place the important news angle of the lead in the main clause of the sentence, and the lesser aspects of the story in subordinate clauses.

All violations of this rule produce unemphatic and distorted leads, such as this one:

> City Manager Frank Gibson charged Greensburg Council members with "self interest" and "political cowardice" when he resigned today.

This lead leaves the reader puzzled. "Did Gibson really resign?" he asks himself. Then he goes back and reads the sentence again.

The problem here is that the important news has been placed in a subordinate clause and, accordingly, *de-*emphasized, while the less important material is given top billing. Confusion could have been eliminated by keeping the news in the main clause:

City Manager Frank Gibson resigned today, charging Greensburg Council members with "self interest" and "political cowardice."

Any lead that must be read twice for understanding is a poor lead.

Other Considerations in Lead Writing

Up to this point, we have been dealing with the essential requirements for vigorous and emphatic news leads. There are occasions, however, when even more is required, or at least a variation of the basic rules.

Every issue of a newspaper contains stories that, while weak in news value or social significance, more than make up for this shortcoming in humor, irony or human interest appeal. Such stories require special treatment and will be discussed in a later chapter.

Apart from considerations of style and emphasis, certain technical problems also arise in the writing of leads from the fundamental requirement that news writing be clear and accurate as well as emphatic. Most of these problems fall into two general areas: *attribution* and *identification*.

Attribution

Even a cursory examination of leads in a newspaper will turn up statements that simply would not be news unless spoken by someone in authority.

For instance, a street-corner evangelist preaching the imminent destruction of the world is unlikely to send reporters running to their typewriters. But should a geophysicist reach a similar conclusion, after reporting on his studies of the ozone layer covering the atmosphere, his comments will be picked up by every wire service and relayed from coast to coast.

This phenomenon, of course may only reflect our current preference for scientific rather than religious authority, but it serves to underscore the fact that the statement itself, without a *recognized* authority behind it is not news.

The specific task of the journalist, then, is to determine which stories require this authority to be newsworthy and which do not, and to write his leads accordingly. Linking the newsworthy statement to an authority is called *attribution.*

In most cases, a proper name is not necessary for attribution in the lead:

> Optimistic business forecasts by the President's Council of Economic Advisers were sharply disputed by a Harvard Business School economist.

Here, a general description of the authority is perfectly adequate to support the lead statement. The economist's name, which would not be familiar to most readers, can be used in the second paragraph.

In some instances, however, and especially in stories based on statistics or highly controversial statements, the proper names should appear in the lead, as in this example from the *Washington Post:*

> Median family income rose 7 percent to $12,840 last year, the Census Bureau reported yesterday, but prices increased even more.

Or in this from the *Philadelphia Inquirer:*

> WASHINGTON—Former Defense Secretary Clark M. Clifford, one of the godfathers of the Central Intelligence Agency, has charged that the agency he helped create has

been running wild, in violation of both its own charter and the
U. S. Constitution.

In the first example, the Census Bureau is the most authoritative source for the statement and should, therefore, be identified. Note that the attribution has been tucked inconspicuously in the middle of the sentence, giving prime emphasis to the findings.

The second example is an instance where the authority is the news: Clark Clifford, a nationally-prominent figure who served as an adviser to several Presidents, is attacking the CIA, an agency he helped to establish. Thus, the name moves to the front of the lead.

Reporters covering public affairs, in City Hall or in Washington, D. C., often will obtain important stories from persons in authority who, for one reason or another, cannot be identified. If he believes that his informant is trustworthy, the reporter will use the story and attribute it in the lead to "an informed source" or "a high official."

We shall take up the practical questions of attribution, especially in connection with stories built around speeches or direct quotations, in a later chapter.

Identification

Another technical problem that arises in lead writing is that of identification. Stated in its simplest terms, the problem is this: how does the writer identify each person, place or organization mentioned in the lead so that its connection with the news is immediately apparent to the reader.

At first glance, this may appear to be a minor problem. But when it is done poorly or not at all, the story is impaired and the reader finds himself asking, "I wonder if that's the same Tom Bradley who . . . ?"

Adequate identification is always relative to the degree of prominence of the subject and, in some instances, to past prominence of which the reading public may no longer be aware. In the latter case, it becomes the duty of the reporter to refresh the public memory.

Let us take for example an ordinary traffic accident in which the victim, Richard Williams, is critically injured. To identify the man in the lead simply as "Richard Williams" would be inadequate, since in the newspaper's circulation area there may be a dozen or more men named Richard Williams.

The only way to adequately identify the victim would be to include his full name with middle initial—if obtainable—his age and home address. Thus, his newspaper identity becomes "Richard A. Williams, 57, of 2239 Chestnut St." All three elements must appear as a unit, not separately inserted into the story.

Let us suppose, however, that in checking out the story, we find that Williams is a well-known trial lawyer and a former district attorney. This degree of prominence requires that we identify him in the lead in the terms that he is known to most readers. Our story, then, would begin:

> Richard A. Williams, a widely-known trial lawyer and a former Philadelphia district attorney, was critically injured last night when he was struck by a car near 7th and Walnut Sts.

While the subject's home address should appear high in the story, it is no longer crucial to identity.

The business of identification becomes more complex when we are dealing with persons who are prominent in more than one sphere of activity. An actress who has championed political and social causes, a businessman who is equally well-known as a civic leader, or a scholar whose expertise spans several areas of learning—all present problems for the lead writer.

To identify a multi-faceted personality in one phrase requires that we single out two or three of the subject's best known areas of activity and hold back others for later in the story.

The problem becomes most acute in writing leads for obituaries where a lifetime of activity must be summed up in a single phrase. Such a problem faced the *New York Times* on

Aug. 3, 1972, when it received word of the death of Paul Goodman.

The *Times'* obituary by Michael T. Kaufman, published the following day, pointed out that books written by Goodman were listed in the catalogue of the New York Public Library "under 21 different categories, ranging from fiction to education to poetry to applied linguistics to drama to United States Constitutional law."

The obituary also noted that Goodman was "a practicing psychotherapist, a lecturer on all the things he wrote about, a pacifist anarchist who willingly picketed and demonstrated for many causes and a frequent contributor to magazines and literary journals."

How can a career of such diversity be crammed into a single phrase? The *Times* used this lead for its obituary:

> NORTH STRATFORD, N. H., Aug. 3—Paul Goodman, the writer, therapist and social critic who has been called the father figure of the New Left, died here at his farm last night after suffering his third heart attack. He was 60 years old.

To identify Goodman to its readers, the *Times* chose three broad areas of the man's activity, then added a characterization based on his writings and political activism during the 60s. The final "father figure" image adds a dynamic dimension to the identity and accurately describes a position that Goodman held in the eyes of many readers.

In other kinds of writing, the nature of the story will usually determine which attributes are selected for identification in the lead.

For the sake of illustration, let us suppose that we receive a news release from a local environmental organization announcing a forthcoming lecture on the subject of ocean pollution.

The lecturer, we learn, is a man who has been a chemist, a marine biologist, a diver and underwater explorer, and an author of several books on environmental subjects.

If we recognize among the list of books, one that was widely publicized, we might say in the lead:

> Roger Miller, marine biologist and author of "The Silent Sea," will speak on the threat of ocean pollution at . . .

If, instead, his books were all of a technical nature, we might begin:

> Roger Miller, marine biologist and underwater explorer, will speak on . . .

By using a compound identification we imply that Miller's authority as a lecturer is broader than that of a scientific specialist, which, of course, is true. In either case, any relevant background not used in the lead would be inserted later in the story.

When preparing a story that follows up an earlier news account, it is important for the writer to identify the persons involved in terms of the previous story:

> James Dean, an eight-year-old Greensburg boy who was critically injured April 5 in a freak playground accident, died today at Memorial Hospital.

To identify the boy as "James Dean, 8, son of Mr. and Mrs. Edward F. Dean, 121 E. Elm St." would obscure the news, which is not that an eight-year-old boy died, but that *the boy who was injured at the playground two weeks ago* died. Persons who read the earlier story are likely to remember the incident but not the name of the victim.

The lead from the *Philadelphia Inquirer* used earlier to illustrate a point of attribution also shows how a carefully chosen figure of speech can add subtle meaning to an identifying phrase:

> WASHINGTON—Former Defense Secretary Clark M. Clifford, one of the *godfathers* of the Central Intelligence Agency, has charged . . .

Here the word "godfather" is used metaphorically to suggest a far more intimate connection than would be expressed by the word "founder."

Figures of speech should be used sparingly in identification, as in other areas of writing. They can be justified only in stories featuring personalities already well-known to the readers. In using figures, the writer is not dispensed from his obligation to be accurate; the figure must fit the facts and its effect on the reader must be the one intended.

Organizations whose names give no clue to their function also should be adequately identified in the lead. It is almost meaningless to write:

> James McDonnell, an area real estate broker, has been elected president of the Citizens Action Committee.

The news comes into focus only when the organization is properly identified as "a group vehemently opposed to public housing."

Whether concerned with persons, places or organizations, effective identification describes the subject in such a way that the reader can quickly establish its relationship to the news.

4 : DEVELOPING
THE STORY

Having constructed a lead sentence that simply and emphatically expresses the most important aspects of the news, the writer finds himself already one jump ahead in the process of developing the story. If the lead brings the news into sharp focus, the rest of the story seems to flow naturally from it.

The writer's next task is to provide other significant information that could not be included in the lead. In accident stories, this means identifying the victims. In reports on legislative bodies, it means summing up other pertinent actions not described in the lead. In stories based on statistics, it could mean citing exceptions to overall trends.

This part of a news story is often referred to as the "secondary lead," and its purpose is to permit material of importance to be inserted high in the story before a detailed elaboration of the lead material is begun.

Most newspaper readers are unaware of the device, even though it often breaks the continuity of the story. Yet it serves their interest by acquainting them at the outset with the major aspects of the news event.

Here is an example from the Associated Press:

> NEW YORK—Police searched for suspects and clues yesterday in the bombings of banks, government buildings and corporate towers in New York, Chicago and Washington.
>
> A Puerto Rican separatist group claimed it set the explosions in all three cities to attack "Yanki government" and "capitalist institutions." At the same time, however, an anonymous telephone caller said a Washington blast was linked to

a US "sellout of Israel." The explosion came on the day Egypt's President Anwar Sadat visited President Ford.

The blasts, which occurred in the three cities within 47 minutes of each other, from 1:43 a.m. to 2:30 a.m. EST, caused no injuries.

There were five bombs in New York City . . .

In the above example, the third paragraph flows naturally from the lead sentence. But the author, judging the material in the second paragraph too important to wait until later, has interrupted the normal flow of the story to make it a secondary lead.

In other cases, the second paragraph of the story will be used for background material or historical data necessary for a full understanding of the lead, as in the following example from the *New York Times:*

WASHINGTON, Sept. 15—The Senate Select Committee on Intelligence has heard testimony that the Central Intelligence Agency transferred poison to an African outpost for use in killing Patrice Lumumba, the Congolese leader, but that the poison was never administered, sources familiar with the testimony said today.

Mr. Lumumba was deposed as Premier of the Congo (now called Zaire) in December, 1960, and was taken as a prisoner to Leopoldville. On Feb. 9, 1961, the Central Government announced that he had escaped with two companions, and on Feb. 13 it said Mr. Lumumba had been murdered by Congolese tribesmen.

The testimony about poison . . .

In simpler stories, especially those based on single incidents, a secondary lead may not be necessary. Nevertheless, in scanning their notes, news writers should remain alert to the possibility of a secondary lead.

When this primary obligation to the reader has been discharged, the writer then is free to develop the major issues raised in the lead. It is precisely at this point in the story that many beginners start to waver. Having written an acceptable lead, they tend to fall back on organizational devices learned in English classes, such as climactic and chronological order.

In news writing, however, the organizational method that applies to the story as a whole also applies to each part of the story, and that method is *order of importance*. The same critical stance that enables a writer to scan all of his material and construct an effective lead must be maintained throughout the story. Thus, the development of the lead begins with the most important part of the lead.

Let us take an example. In the last chapter we used the following lead to demonstrate the principle of subordination:

> City Manager Frank Gibson resigned today, charging Greensburg Council members with "self interest" and "political cowardice."

Let us assume that the story does not require a secondary lead. Our next task, then, is to begin an elaboration of the major news. If our lead accurately emphasizes the important aspect of the story, we already have a clue as to where to begin. We begin by developing the material in the main clause of the lead.

In the story at hand, this means that the circumstances of Gibson's resignation must be explained first and then his comments about city officials. Thus, the second paragraph of this story might read like this:

> Gibson announced his resignation at a hastily-arranged press conference at City Hall. Speaking informally to reporters, he explained his action by reading from a letter he had sent to City Council.

Having amplified the fact of the resignation, the writer now is free to deal with the substance of Gibson's remarks. But first he must explain those comments which were quoted briefly in the lead. The reader deserves an explanation of Gibson's attack on the council. So we might continue in this fashion:

> In his letter of resignation, Gibson said he had "labored unceasingly for more than a year to do those things that must be done to give the city a sound fiscal structure."
>
> "I was blocked at every turn by council members who placed their own self interest above the good of the city," he

said. "In 24 years of public service I have rarely seen political cowardice so widespread in one legislative body."

Gibson was referring to his failure to obtain the support of a majority of council members for a controversial tax package that he had repeatedly described as essential for the economic health of the city.

The tax package would have included a new five per cent sales tax on non-food items and a one mill increase in the city's real estate tax rate.

At this point in the story we have satisfied the expectations of the reader that were aroused by our lead. We now can turn to other remarks of interest made by Gibson at his press conference. Again, order of importance continues to be the rule, not the order in which Gibson made the comments:

Gibson warned that Greensburg faced a bleak period ahead unless residents were willing to face its problems honestly and demand that their elected representatives take action.

"The future of Greensburg now rests in the hands of its citizens," Gibson declared. "If residents are willing to rise above their own petty concerns and demand nothing less from their councilmen, there is no reason why the problems of this city cannot be surmounted."

Gibson said his resignation would be effective April 1, one month from the date of his letter to council.

He said he planned to take a two-week vacation in the Bahamas before making any plans for the future, but he disclosed that he was considering several offers of employment from municipalities along the eastern seaboard.

The story might include background information on Gibson: when he was appointed, what he had done before coming to Greensburg, etc. It might also contain reactions to the resignation by council members, if they can be obtained. But that is not our primary concern here. Our point is that the story must be ordered consciously and continually by the writer along a descending spiral of importance that flows directly from the lead.

In covering speeches by prominent personalities, the writer

often will be tempted to follow the speaker's order. He must resist this temptation by reminding himself that he is working with a different audience and in a different medium, and that these factors are paramount in determining order.

There are times when a chronology of events may be important to the understanding of a story, but it should be stressed that, even then, chronology is merely a part of the story, not an ordering device.

To construct a news story by following order of importance requires some effort on the part of the journalist if he is to obtain smooth continuity in his writing and impart a feeling of organic wholeness to the story. He must prepare the reader for each shift of thought, so that it appears to flow naturally from that which preceded it, and he must include necessary background information without diminishing the reader's interest in the progress of the story.

We shall turn now to an examination of those techniques that will assist the writer in this task.

THE FRACTURED PARAGRAPH

In English classes, students learn that the paragraph is the primary unit of composition and that its purpose is to fully develop a single thought. It contains a topic sentence which expresses that thought and other sentences which expand and elaborate it.

In addition, the paragraph is given a visual unity. Each new paragraph is indented from the left margin, so that the reader is made aware that a new thought is being introduced at that point.

All well and good. But when we attempt to carry over the composition class rules for paragraphing into news writing, a problem arises. A newspaper column is at the most only about 2¼ inches wide. When an average paragraph of three or four sentences is set in a newspaper column, it becomes a forbidding mass of gray type that severely tests a reader's patience.

So that while maintaining the internal criteria of a good

paragraph—unity, order, coherence and completeness—the journalist breaks the visual unity by indenting whenever the indention will aid readability. He may indent after the first sentence of a new paragraph if it runs more than three typewritten lines, since an average line of typewritten copy equals approximately two lines of type in a newspaper column.

To the student fresh out of an English composition class, newspaper paragraphing may appear to be capricious, but it is not. A closer examination will show that the journalist, in shattering the visual unity of the traditional paragraph, nevertheless has observed the basic rules for paragraphing, often to an even greater degree than other writers who have the built-in unity of the visual paragraph to lean on.

Let us look at the following story from United Press International:

> WASHINGTON—The House voted yesterday, 298 to 106, to end for future members of the armed services the GI education program which helped veterans of World War II and subsequent conflicts complete their schooling.
>
> The action came despite opposition led by Reps. Robert Edgar (D., Pa.), and Robert Cornell (D., Wis.), who argued that the programs were just as essential for peacetime GIs as for those who fought for the nation.
>
> The bill, sent to the Senate, would not affect military and former military personnel entitled to the benefits. It contains a nine-month extension to help some of these complete graduate training.
>
> However, persons entering service after Dec. 31, 1975, would not be eligible.
>
> They would continue to acquire eligibility for Veterans Administration-guaranteed home loans. Moreover, some veterans of the period between World War II and the Korean War would become eligible for such loans.
>
> President Ford recommended the educational cutoff when he proclaimed the end of the Vietnam War May 7, 1975.
>
> Proponents argued that the educational program was de-

signed for wartime veterans, especially those whose service interrupted their education.

The end of hostilities and of the peacetime draft and the voluntary military services eliminate the program's need, they said.

Opponents said the House should consider continuing some benefits.

The bill is estimated to save $1.1 billion over the next five years.

At first glance, the story seems to be ten paragraphs long. When we look more closely, however, and apply the traditional criteria for a paragraph, we shall find only four.

The lead and the second paragraph, which forms a secondary lead, are in reality one traditional paragraph dealing with the action of the House of Representatives.

The third, fourth and fifth paragraphs of the story make up another paragraph explaining the effect of the legislation on military personnel and former servicemen.

The sixth, seventh and eighth paragraphs of the story are one complete paragraph describing the supporters and opponents of the legislation.

The ninth paragraph in one sentence introduces a new thought which is not further developed.

Thus, behind the frequent indentions which break up the long mass of type, we can find the unmistakable presence of the traditional paragraph form. Only its visual unity has been altered.

The "fractured paragraph" of news writing, which is designed primarily to aid the reader, also serves the purposes of the copy desk by permitting new information to be added to a story or sections deleted with little or no resetting of type.

Nevertheless, this technique places certain obligations on the writer who must at the same time maintain an orderly and coherent development of ideas. He must connect the sentences which develop each idea in such a way that their essential unity is perceived by the reader, even though the visual form has been broken.

To do so, the writer relies on three basic devices: key words, transitional words and phrases, and pronoun references.

Key Words

Since, in news writing, an indention is no longer a clue to a shift in thought, the writer must provide another signal to the reader that a new idea-paragraph is beginning. An effective way to do this is to choose a key word or phrase related to the new idea and place it at the beginning of the sentence.

The key word, thus, breaks the continuity of the preceding thought, but at the same time points back to an earlier statement in the story which now is being developed.

In the following example from the Associated Press, the key words and phrases have been italicized:

> PASADENA, Cal. (AP)—A massive development effort by the auto industry and the government could put a smogless, gas-saving engine on the road by 1985, according to a study financed by the Ford Motor Co.
>
> *A team of scientists* from the Jet Propulsion laboratory released its report yesterday, saying the 18-month, $500,000 study was independent of any industry influence.
>
> *Cars* using the new engines would virtually cease to be sources of pollution, said Dr. R. Rhoads Stephenson, head of the 20-member team.
>
> *The engines* could run on various liquid fuels so efficiently that the nation's energy consumption by automobiles would be cut by 30 to 45 per cent, he said.
>
> At current gasoline prices this would mean an annual savings of $8 billion or more, he said.
>
> *These benefits* would make the five-to-seven-year, $1 billion development program well worth the effort, said Stephenson, whose team studied nine types of engines in the U. S., Europe and Japan.

"If the price of fuel stays high or goes higher, and gas availability remains a problem, the industry might decide to pursue this course voluntarily," he said. But the high cost of development probably would have to be underwritten in part by the federal government, he said.

There was no immediate comment from Ford or other car makers or the government.

Ford, like the other manufacturers, is currently committed to the conventional internal combustion engine, but Ford funded the study "because they've been under pressure from Congress and other people in Washington to make a transition to a new type of engine," Stephenson said in an interview.

The study team settled on two designs for the engine of the future, both in existence now but not ready for production. The Brayton gas turbine and the Stirling engine should be developed simultaneously until one proves superior, the scientists recommended.

The Brayton makes use of compressed gas that is forced through a turbine wheel to turn a drive shaft.

In the Stirling engine, a burner heats a compressed gas that is piped to cylinders containing pistons, which in turn cause a wobble plate to rotate the drive shaft.

In the above story, the skillful placement of key words alerts the reader to each shift of thought.

Transitional Words and Phrases

Another device that can be used to assist readers in following the development of a complex story is the use of transitional words and phrases—words or groups of words that explicitly indicate the relationship of one idea to another.

When used at the beginning of a sentence, connectives, such as "Meanwhile," "Nevertheless," "As a result," or "In a related action," provide smooth continuity between the elements of a story. It should be noted that such phrases can be used either to introduce a new idea or to link together statements developing a single idea.

In the following report on Soviet-American relations in the *Baltimore Sun,* we can see how the use of transitional words and phrases (italicized) can give added coherence to a story based primarily on analysis:

WASHINGTON—The prospects for a new Soviet-United States arms agreement and a Washington summit meeting this year have fallen to near zero, with important political implications for both sides.

Some officials fear the whole process of detente could be endangered. Others fear Soviet-American relations might be hopelessly distorted in the U.S. presidential campaign next year.

For the record, the Soviet leadership now has in hand the latest U.S. proposal for a 10-year strategic arms limitation accord. Even American officials do not expect Moscow to accept it.

Without agreement, most administration sources say, Leonid I. Brezhnev, the Soviet leader, cannot make his long-delayed trip to Washington. *In fact,* a visit without an arms accord appears to be ruled out by both sides because of Mr. Brezhnev's domestic pressures and the probable attitude of the U.S. Congress.

Earlier this week Soviet officials told a Western correspondent that an arms agreement might be reached in January. *But* "they're just guessing," an American specialist said, "making the point that we're not going to get it this year."

Apart from the substance of the arms talks, the schedules of both Mr. Ford and Mr. Brezhnev are becoming crowded. "There's a week available to the President right after the middle of November," a U.S. diplomat noted, "but I see no hope of getting SALT settled by then."

Right after that Mr. Ford is expected to spend almost two weeks in China and other Asian countries. In December, Mr. Brezhnev has a series of important trips on his schedule.

At some point in this sequence the dynamics of domestic politics in both countries are expected to come into play more visibly than they have so far.

The use of transitional phrases can also be effective in reporting the meetings of public bodies where many disparate actions must be combined in a single, coherent story.

In those instances where the shift of thought is unusually abrupt, or where the introduction of a new topic may require background information, a transitional paragraph should be written.

Pronoun References

One of the simplest ways of maintaining coherence within the "fractured paragraph" of news writing is to use pronouns, whenever possible, in referring back to the subject of the topic sentence.

This may seem obvious to writers who do this as a matter of course, but it nevertheless requires that the subject of the topic sentence be maintained as the subject of the sentences which develop it.

Thus, if in the course of a story we were to say:

> Mayor Livingston warned that unless drastic cost-cutting procedures were adopted in all departments during the coming fiscal year, the city would face an "unmanageable" financial crisis.

We can gain maximum coherence in developing this thought by keeping the mayor as the subject of the sentences that follow and using a pronoun reference:

> *He* said *he* had spoken informally to many department heads about budgetary cutbacks but without any apparent effect.
>
> *He* emphasized, however, that there was no reason for panic as long as city officials and Council were willing to support *his* proposals.

By using this device, the essential thought paragraph remains a coherent unit, even though broken into three paragraphs of type. Pronoun references can be used just as effectively with places, things, published statements and other non-personal nouns.

INFORMATION WEAVING

Another technical problem that confronts the journalist who is attempting to write a coherent and interesting news account is the need to provide enough necessary details and background information to make the story fully understandable to the reader.

Many beginners fail in the attempt because they are unable to put themselves in the place of the reader. They write, instead, from the privileged position of one who is fully acquainted with the facts. The result is a story full of gaps that leaves the reader perplexed and irritated.

Once aware of the problem, though, beginning writers usually run to the other extreme; that is, they are likely to write paragraphs of solid information that bring the forward movement of the story to an abrupt halt. A series of these "information breaks" will diminish the interest of even an avid reader.

The ideal solution is to insert the necessary details and background information into the story in such a way that the movement never stops. This can be done by "weaving in" such material in subordinate clauses while reserving the main clauses for the progress of the story. There may be times when this cannot be done, but they will be rare if the writer is aware of his duty to maintain interest and constructs his sentences and paragraphs accordingly.

In the following fragment from an Associated Press story on former U. S. Attorney General John Mitchell's appearance before the Senate Intelligence Committee we can see how a considerable amount of background information (italicized here) can be woven into a single paragraph without stopping the movement of the story:

> Helms testified earlier this week that he told Mitchell about the mail openings in 1971.

> Mitchell, *who testified in closed session before the committee several weeks ago,* had sworn that he was told only about mail covers, *a legal procedure for photographing the outside of envelopes*—not mail openings, according to chief counsel F.A.O. Schwarz.

To see what happens when this practice is not followed, let us rewrite the second paragraph:

> Mitchell testified in closed session before the committee several weeks ago. He had sworn that he was told only about mail covers, not mail openings, according to chief counsel F.A.O. Schwarz. Mail covers are a legal procedure for photographing the outside of envelopes.

Writers should be aware that any sentence used solely to provide background information breaks the continuity of the story. Accordingly, they should make every effort to provide this information within the framework of a sentence that moves the story forward.

ENDING THE STORY

If we carry the analogy of the "inverted pyramid" to its geometric conclusion, we find that the form ultimately narrows down to a point at which it ends.

So also do most news stories. After dealing with the major facets of the news, the story turns to minor details, and when these have been exhausted, it trails to an end.

This is the normal procedure, and with most of the routine news that passes through a newspaper, it is the only feasible one. Yet, from time to time, the writer will find himelf involved in a news story that, for one reason or another, suggests a deliberate ending.

It might be the presence of a particularly striking direct quote that sums up the essence of the story, or it might be simply a statement of fact that provides an ironic but accurate perspective on the news. In either case, the writer is justified in using the material for an ending, as long as the main news section of the story is not harmed as a result.

The ending obviously cannot be a comment by the writer. Nor can it be a punch-line that appears strained or redundant. It is a completion to the story brought about by placing at the end a particularly telling fact or quote. When it is skillfully done, an ending will enhance any story.

The following example of a deliberate ending is taken from an Associated Press story on the resignation of the Rev. William Sloane Coffin, Jr., as chaplain of Yale University.

Noting that the Rev. Mr. Coffin was not stepping down from his widely known role as a political activist, the story goes on to describe the minister's involvement in the civil rights and peace movements after leaving a job with the CIA in the mid-1950s.

It closes with these paragraphs:

> He was at the center of the massive May Day 1970 demonstration in New Haven and was credited along with others for its relatively peaceful conclusion. A visitor to Hanoi in 1972 to view war damage, he recently turned his efforts to the worldwide war on hunger.
>
> "Fifteen years from now we're going to be a very different country," the Rev. Mr. Coffin said recently. "It's either going to be grim and mean or it really can be a little more courageous, quite imaginative and a lot more compassionate."

Whenever he is handling a story of more than routine significance, the writer should remain alert for the possibility of a strong ending and scan his notes for appropriate material.

5 : THE ESSENTIALS OF NEWS STYLE

In earlier chapters, we have emphasized the power of various media and inventions to shape the language of news writing. This phenomenon should not be viewed as peculiar to journalism. Technological force is at work in all historical eras on all kinds of writing, but it is only in periods of rapid change, such as the 19th century, that it becomes more easily perceptible.

The invention of movable type in the 15th century radically altered the printing process and, ultimately, the kind of writing that would pass through it. There can be little doubt that the luxuriant writing styles that flourished during the next 400 years owed as much to Gutenberg's invention as they did to any author's originality.

Prior to this breakthrough, writing that would appear in book form must first be carved by hand on page-sized wooden blocks for printing. Given the arduous and time-consuming nature of this process, it is no wonder that few authors, other than the Divinity, were considered worthy enough for its application.

Movable type broke the bottleneck of printing technology and, in the process, created the "writer"—the man who writes for an audience of readers. Looking back at the literature that followed, it seems almost as if its authors, intoxicated by the power of the new medium, spilled out word upon word in lavish abandon.

Jonathan Swift, writing more than 200 years after Gutenberg, was filled with this exuberant spirit as he opened his essay on "The Art of Political Lying":

We are told the Devil is the father of lies, and was a liar from the beginning; so that, beyond contradiction, the invention is old; and, which is more, his first essay of it was purely political, employed in undermining the authority of his prince, and seducing a third part of the subjects from their obedience: for which he was driven down from heaven, where (as Milton expresses it) he had been viceroy of a great western province; and forced to exercise his talent in inferior regions among other fallen spirits, poor or deluded men, whom he still daily tempts to his own sin, and will ever do so, till he be chained in the bottomless pit.

An extreme example, but it is not untypical of an English prose style that pushed syntax and sentence structure to the utmost limits, piling clause on clause, figure on figure, and withholding the main idea for use as a climactic ending.

This extravagant style persisted well into the 19th century; even Charles Dickens, writing in 1859, was not immune, as his often-quoted opening to *A Tale of Two Cities* indicates:

It was the best of times, it was the worst of times, it was the age of wisdom, it was the age of foolishness, it was the epoch of belief, it was the epoch of incredulity, it was the season of Light, it was the season of Darkness, it was the spring of hope, it was the winter of despair, we had everything before us, we had nothing before us, we were all going direct to heaven, we were all going direct the other way—in short, the period was so far like the present period, that some of its noisiest authorities insisted on its being received, for good or for evil, in the superlative degree of comparison only.

The best writers of this period, like Dickens, gave a vigor and clarity to the style by their deft choice of words and by arranging clauses in such a way that the length of the sentence did not necessarily diminish its coherence.

But the force that would ultimately curtail expansive prose was not a new school of writers, but a new environment created by the exigencies of the telegraph press.

The emergence of the electric telegraph as the prime transmitter of news meant that a new technological bottle-neck had been placed on the craft of writing. And, as we noted in Chapter 2, journalists working within the environment of the telegraph press would be compelled to observe its strictures.

Style, therefore, is not an arbitrary set of rules for writing based on a consensus of English teachers, but a discipline that arises from the necessity of communicating with a reader through a particular medium.

This conception of style does not rule out originality or inventiveness on the part of the writer. Even while adhering closely to the discipline of the craft, good writers have managed to find their own unique modes of expression. The sonnet is one of the most rigorously controlled forms of poetry, and yet every major poet who used the form, from William Shakespeare to Elizabeth Barrett Browning, left an indelible personal mark upon it.

Newspaper style has evolved into its present form over the past 150 years. It has been shaped by the telegraph, the typewriter, the telephone and other 19th century inventions, and it still is changing in response to the new electronic technology of our own time.

Essentially, it is a writing style geared to reach the widest possible audience through the medium of the daily newspaper. The emergence of new journalistic forms, such as the city and regional magazines and the new urban weeklies, are modifying the basic style, but mainly in terms of structure. In these new publications, the "inverted pyramid" rarely can be seen. But at the sentence and paragraph level, the writing exhibits all of the characteristics of contemporary newspaper style.

Although we write in a time of profound change among print media, it is fairly safe to predict that the newspaper style which reached its maturity after the advent of electronic media, will remain the basic language of journalism for some time to come.

Contemporary news style is simple, direct and vigorous. For the sake of clarity, it is biased in favor of the simple declarative sentence, but with enough variation to avoid monotony. Its sentences are built around the noun and the verb, and all other words and phrases must contribute tellingly to that central relationship or be struck out. Finally, since it seeks to reach a broad spectrum of readers, it uses words that are short, descriptive and non-technical.

In brief, it is a writing style admirably suited to the needs of human communication in a world that often seems bent on frustrating them. And in the hands of an expert writer, it can be at times powerful, moving, and even elegant.

To look more closely at the elements of this style, we shall examine it under its two most important aspects: the choice of words and the structure of sentences.

THE CHOICE OF WORDS

Brevity may or may not be "the soul of wit," but ever since the marriage of the electric telegraph and the daily newspaper, it has been an essential component of journalistic writing. Later, as photography entered the newspaper, taking space away from words, and, finally, radio and television appeared as alternatives to print, the emphasis on brevity became an overriding consideration.

In the electronic age, redundancy has a double meaning for journalists working in the print media. It means that they must avoid not only repeating themselves, but also repeating what has been done—and possibly done better—by radio and television.

Today's reader, who is also a viewer and a listener, has less time for print media. But when he turns to print, as he must when he seeks information and understanding that he cannot obtain elsewhere, he expects to find it in a form that is both succinct and interesting.

In using the words "brevity" and "succinct," we do not necessarily refer to an absolute measurement of length. We mean essentially that the writer's ideas and information be presented as simply and as effectively as possible. This notion of brevity, then, can be applied to long articles as well as to short ones.

To write in a manner that is both succinct and interesting, the journalist must begin at the level of words. If interest and brevity are paramount, then each word must justify its place in the sentence or be replaced by a better one, or, if unnecssary, be eliminated.

Governing all choices, of course, is the fundamental rule of accuracy which requires that the word evoke in the reader the exact meaning intended by the writer. But we all know that writing can be accurate and dull, or accurate and verbose, or—as is more often the case—all three. Journalistic writing, which seeks to capture and engage a previously uninterested reader, demands that accuracy be fused with interest and bevity.

So for journalists, the choice comes down to this: among several words, all of which may be accurate, which one contributes most to brevity, vividness and understanding by most readers?

We shall look now at four categories of words, among which the best writers are likely to make this choice.

Short Words

Considering the journalistic stress on brevity, it is not surprising that news writers, given a choice, will pick the shortest word. But that is not the only reason.

It turns out that in the English language the shortest words are usually the most familiar and, therefore, the most easily understood by a wide range of readers. But there is an even more compelling reason for using short words.

In English, most short words are of Anglo-Saxon origin. They are words like "home," "friend," "land" and "drunk," and they contain far greater emotional power than their equivalents of Latin derivation, which, in the above case, would be "domicile," "acquaintance," "nation," and "inebriated." In addition to being long, Latin-root words tend to be abstract and emotionally detached.

Thus, it is not only in the interest of brevity that a journalist chooses a short word over a long one to express the same idea. The emotional connotations of short, Anglo-Saxon words make them a potent device for adding strength and vigor to writing, and the journalist who wishes to communicate vividly to his readers will find that he must use them as the basis of his language.

The following front-page lead from the *New York Post* deals with events in New York City's complex financial crisis. Despite its considerable length, the lead is clear and forceful because the writer has chosen short, strong words to dramatize the action:

> WASHINGTON—The New York police and fire unions, angered by the treatment they have received from Gov. Carey and Major Beame during the city's fiscal crisis, have decided to flex their muscles to halt future layoffs and even restore some already dismissed men to their jobs.

The reliance on short, familiar words in no way detracts from the literary quality of writing. It is a mark of pretentiousness in a writer to seek out longer and more complex words when short ones will do.

Winston Churchill, the British statesman, was a master of the English language in its spoken and written forms. He wrote a four-volume history of the English-speaking peoples and a six-volume history of World War II, in which he played so critical a role. Yet, he is best remembered for four, short Anglo-Saxon words that rallied Britain against the Nazis: "blood, toil, tears and sweat."

Concrete Words

It has always been true that writing which permits the reader to see, hear or feel the events described communicates with greater intensity than that which speaks in abstract or general terms. But this fact takes on added significance in our own time. Contemporary readers, who are accustomed to receiving a large share of their information through television, radio, film and photography, have come to expect from the printed word a vividness that at least approaches the sensory power of these newer media.

There can be no excuse today for writing that is dull, vague or uninteresting. Aware of the pressure of electronic media on the printed word, many weeklies are staking out impressive circulation territories—even in urban areas— by providing vigorous writing that meets the expectations of modern readers.

What follows is the opening of an article by Jack Newfield in the *Village Voice:*

> After riots, earthquakes, and floods, there are usually a few self-possessed cynics who take advantage of the chaos and loot the ruins.
>
> This is beginning to happen now in New York City. After a season of job layoffs, near-default, a school strike, a wage freeze, a reduction of services, and a higher transit fare, a group of politicians and corporation executives are about to pull off a deal that will deprive this insolvent city of more than $50 million over the next ten years. The deal will benefit two of the biggest financial institutions in the world—the Gulf + Western conglomerate and Chase Manhattan Bank. And Mayor Beame and Deputy Mayor Cavanaugh know about it— they are even pushing it.
>
> Last Wednesday at 5 p.m. . . .

This, of course, is the lead-in to a feature article about an intricate financial maneuver, but Newfield has approached it in such concrete terms and with such vivid imagery, that the reader is drawn immediately into the story.

Writers who wish to communicate effectively in an environment dominated by electronic media must choose words that are concrete and specific, especially those which evoke a sensory response in the reader.

In the third chapter we saw how this principle can be applied in the selection of verbs. But it applies equally to nouns and adjectives.

Nouns should be as specific as the context allows. We do not say, "Police found a gun in the victim's overnight bag," when, in fact, the "gun" was a .38 caliber revolver.

Since the noun and the verb carry the major burden of communication in news writing, the adjective is used sparingly, and Mark Twain's rule still applies: "When in doubt, strike it out." When necessary, adjectives should be chosen with care and precision.

The use of the word "very" is always a tip-off that a weak or imprecise adjective has been chosen. To say of a man that he was "a very good photographer" is the sign of a lazy writer. He could be an "expert photographer" or an "award-winning photographer." It is the writer's duty to tell us.

By using concrete and specific words, the writer keeps his ideas in sharp focus and enables the reader to follow the story with a minimum of effort.

Non-technical Words

Every major area of study, from archaeology to zoology, and every profession, trade and technical field has its own distinctive language.

As puzzling as they may appear to the uninitiated, these languages serve a real purpose: they permit persons working within a given sphere of activity to speak to each other with greater precision, speed and clarity. In fact, much of the formal education required for entering a specialized field consists simply of learning the professional language.

The scientific and technological advances of the 20th century, however, have accentuated the problem that specialized languages pose for the journalist. As the one responsible for interpreting scientific gains to the public, the journalist must understand the technical language related to the news, but he must avoid using it when writing his story.

Whenever he functions as an interpreter, whether of science, law, medicine or finance, the journalist is obliged to use the language of his readers, not the jargon of the specialty. This requires that news writers develop the ability to express technical concepts in short, familiar words and to describe complex processes by using analogies that are understandable to the reader.

When technical words are used, as they often must be, they should be explained immediately in simple language.

The problem of translating technical jargon into common language is not faced only by writers who specialize in covering science, medicine or finance. It can arise in almost any story, and every competent writer should be able to cope with it.

The following example, taken from the *New York Post,* shows how a complex physiological process can be made understandable, and even interesting, to the average reader. The example is an excerpt from a story on the case of Karen Anne Quinlan, a 21-year-old woman who at the time of the story had lain in a coma for more than six months and whose parents were seeking court permission to turn off the respirator that was keeping her alive.

After noting that at the time of her collapse Karen had been without a pulse for 30 minutes, the writer goes on to explain the effect:

> This means that whatever caused her coma to begin, the prolonged loss of blood flow to the oxygen-greedy thinking part of the brain must be the cause of the lasting damage. Such anoxia, as it is called, is particularly hard on the cortex of the cerebrum, the crinkled bulging upper brain which is what makes us thinking and communicating humans.

In this example, technical information has been presented so simply and understandably that the reader is unaware of having been given a lesson in physiology. And maybe that is the best test for news writing that attempts to translate information from specialized fields.

The rule against using technical language in news writing also applies to non-technical jargons, such as teen-age slang, Madison Avenue coinages and the inflated speech of bureaucracy known to newsmen as "gobbledegook." Journalists who wish to be understood use standard English in its simplest and most vivid forms.

Unspoiled Words

There is no easier way to kill freshness and vigor in writing than to use words and phrases whose imagery has been dulled by repetition. The reliance on trite words and banal figures is a sign of laziness in a writer, and its effect on the reader is similar to the experience of a diner in a first-class restaurant who is served warmed-over food.

Vigorous writing is fresh and immediate. Writers who produce it choose words with extreme care, building images that fit the ideas they wish to express. Clichés are ready-made images which, even when accurate, give writing a shopworn quality.

So vast is the number of clichés and stale expressions in current usage that even good writers, unless they are vigilant, are likely to include them. It is better to use no figure at all than to say that police "combed the city" looking for suspects, or that residents, threatened by flooding creeks, "worked like Trojans" to build dikes.

The overuse by journalists of words like "launch" and "inaugurate" as substitutes for "begin," warrants their retirement to the areas of shipbuilding and politics, respectively. And expressions like "dull thud," "blunt instrument" and "all-out effort" should simply be retired, period.

THE STRUCTURE OF SENTENCES

All of the techniques cited in Chapter 3 for the construction of an effective lead sentence apply to the writing of good sentences throughout the story. It should be noted, however, that while the lead must be able to stand alone as an independent statement, most sentences in a story serve only to expand and elaborate a previous thought. Their effectiveness, accordingly, is measured more by how well they relate to these other ideas than by any virtues they may possess in isolation.

Thus, within a story, sentence construction is always related to context—the role which the sentence plays in the paragraph. And while our overriding concern no longer is to create a single, emphatic statement, the techniques of word order, voice, verb selection and subordination continue to be the basic tools for sentence building, with only slight modifications.

In the area of word order, the beginning of the sentence continues to be the important position, especially in topic sentences, but now we must also take into account the need for continuity and its demand for smooth transitions. Periodic sentences may be used sparingly to obtain variety and special emphasis.

Active voice remains the essential mode of sentence construction, but writers must remain alert, once the tension of lead writing has relaxed, or they will find themselves using unemphatic passive voice and inactive verb forms.

The selection of strong verbs never ceases to be a fundamental requirement for an effective sentence, but within a story the range of verb choices may be narrowed considerably from those available to the lead writer. It is a good habit for writers to seek alternative forms of the verb ''said,'' but not at the expense of accuracy or simplicity; in most instances, ''stated'' or ''declared'' are pompous synonyms for ''said'' and less effective than a repetition of the latter verb.

From lead to final paragraph, proper subordination of minor sentence elements is the key to clarity and understanding. The skillful use of this technique, however, takes on special importance in the body of the story where the writer seeks variety in his sentence patterns.

Effective subordination permits several ideas to be combined in a sentence, but in such a way that the relationship to the main idea is always clear to the reader. The alternative would be a monotonous succession of short sentences in which each idea is equally emphasized and unrelated to others.

In good news writing, every sentence moves the story forward. When the writer finds that he has written one that does not do this, it is most likely because he has built it on background information or on a minor element that would be more effectively expressed as a subordinate clause in another sentence.

The writer's goal, in short, is to produce, not the perfect sentence, but a pattern of sentences that is cohesive, clear and interesting.

Cohesion ultimately is the product of strong organization, but it can be heightened in writing by the skillful use of connectives and transitional devices. Clarity is obtained by keeping sentence elements properly related to each other through subordination, by the agreement of nouns and verbs, and by accurate pronoun references.

Interest—the hallmark of the professional writer—begins with a constant awareness of the reader and his eccentricities. It overcomes reader inertia by the sheer force of inventiveness and, at the level of the sentence, is expressed by variety, both in sentence length and structure.

The most common problems in sentence writing occur mainly within the second area—that of clarity. And for the sake of convenience they can be grouped into two broad categories: problems that arise from not making clear the relationship of ideas that belong together, and problems that arise from relating ideas that do not belong together.

Faulty Relationships

The sentence error committed most frequently—even by working newspapermen—is the *dangling modifier*. This is a verbal phrase, usually at the beginning of a sentence, that "dangles'' because the subject it purports to modify is either missing or not easily discernible. As a result, the meaning of the sentence is blurred, as in these examples:

> To qualify for the new supervisory positions in the sanitation department, an examination must be passed.

> Having argued against the proposed ordinance, the hearing was recessed and the Mayor left with his aides.

In the first example, the intended subject of the opening phrase is missing altogether from the sentence. When it is inserted correctly, the sentence should read:

> To qualify for the new supervisory positions in the sanitation department, *applicants* must pass an examination.

In the second example, the intended subject is within the sentence, but unrelated to the modifier. To make this relationship clear, the sentence must be rewritten as follows:

> Having argued against the proposed ordinance, the Mayor left with his aides when the hearing was recessed.

Whenever a verbal phrase is used to open a sentence, the writer should check to see that the subject modified immediately follows the phrase.

Another common error in sentence relationships arises from the failure to observe the fundamental rule of *parallelism,* which is that parallel elements should be expressed in parallel form.

In the following example, the parallel elements are *not* expressed in parallel form:

> The newly-established Human Relations Commission has the power to investigate complaints, hold hearings, of subpoenaing witnesses and penalizing violators of the city's fair housing code.

The effect is jarring on the reader. For clarity, the four elements require parallel structure, as follows:

> The newly-established Human Relations Commission has the power to investigate complaints, hold hearings, subpoena witnesses and penalize violators of the city's fair housing code.

Many newsmen who are normally conscientious about observing parallel form err when using the "not only-but" construction. They write:

> To require that each store owner submit proposed external signs and decorations to the art commission for approval would not only be unworkable but uneconomic, witnesses testified.

To be clear, this construction requires that the element following the "not only" be grammatically parallel to the element following the "but." In the example, "not only" is followed by a verb, and "but," by an adjective. A simple transposition restores parallel form:

> To require that each store owner submit proposed external signs and decorations to the art commission for approval would be not only unworkable but uneconomic, witnesses testified.

Writers who seek clarity must avoid all unnecessary changes of perspective within the sentence, especially shifts of subject and voice. A shift of one usually involves a shift of the other.

It is awkward to say:

> The Governor spent a working vacation at Aspen, Colorado, and all of his free time was devoted to skiing.

The sentence can be improved simply by maintaining a single subject:

> The Governor spent a working vacation at Aspen, Colorado, and devoted all of his free time to skiing.

Writers also must be alert to shifts in the voice of verbs within a sentence:

> Senator Jackson sought his party's nomination for President in 1972 but was defeated by George McGovern.

Vigor is retained by keeping all verbs in the active voice:

> Senator Jackson sought his party's nomination for President in 1972 but lost to George McGovern.

Another problem area for writers is the sequence of verb forms in a sentence. The general idea is that all verbs in a sentence should be related to the tense of the main clause, which, in news writing, is normally the past tense.

Yet sentences like these pop up with amazing frequency in even the best newspapers:

> He said he is concerned about the unemployment rate.

> He testified that he wrote the letter because he was angry at the kind of treatment he had received.

The specific rule violated here is the one which requires verbs in subordinate clauses to take the tense of the verb in the main clause. Thus, the first sentence should be written:

> He said he was concerned about the unemployment rate.

Why, then, is the second example incorrect? Because the rule further states that verbs in subordinate clauses which relate to events prior in time to the governing verb must be moved one stage further back in the past.

Accordingly, the second example should take this form:

> He testified that he had written the letter because he had been angry at the kind of treatment he had received.

It should be noted that the last verb in the sequence, "had received," was originally in the past perfect tense. Since there is no tense more remote than past perfect, the verb remains as it was.

The following construction is often used in news writing:

> He wrote the letter, he testified, because he was angry at the kind of treatment he had received.

This form is correct. Here, "he testified" is a parenthetical clause, not the governing verb of the sentence.

The one exception to the rule on sequence of tenses applies when the idea expressed in the subordinate clause is permanently true. It is correct, therefore, to write:

| He said that the diameter of the moon is 2,160 miles. |

Reporting truisms, however, is hardly the business of news writers.

False Relationships

If the purpose of a sentence is to express a single thought, then all of its parts must relate in some way to a central idea. When they do not, sentence unity is destroyed and the reader is confused.

In their singleminded concern for brevity, many beginning writers force together unrelated material and produce sentences like this:

| Born in Des Moines, he was an active trial lawyer, specializing in workmen's compensation cases. |

The reader expects to find a connection between these two ideas. When he cannot, he is annoyed and begins to lose interest in the story.

A subject's place of birth rarely merits a sentence of its own. It should be subordinated in a sentence where a natural relationship can be made, such as:

| Born in Des Moines, he attended public schools in that city and was graduated in 1926 from the State University of Iowa. |

The problem also can arise with parenthetical phrases which, as every writer soon learns, make excellent hiding places for necessary details. In sentences like the following one, this device should not be used:

> Miller, 45, of 225 E. Main St., lifted his attache case and struck the fleeing suspect on the head.

In this example, irrelevant material juxtaposed in a narrative sentence stops the action and spoils the flow of the story.

Both of the above examples are fairly obvious violations of sentence unity. A less obvious but even more common problem is the combining of ideas that seem to be related, yet not closely enough for the reader to see the connection.

The problem is most likely to occur when a news writer, working against a deadline, tries to wrap up a report on a meeting or press conference that includes many disparate topics. He will be tempted to write:

> Councilman Cohen urged residents who supported the proposed zoning ordinance to make known their feelings at the April hearing and announced that sealed bids on sewer construction would be opened at the next council meeting.

Separate ideas belong in separate sentences. Any time saved by the writer in combining them is lost by the reader in trying to figure out the relationship.

6 : QUOTATIONS– THE SPOKEN WORD IN PRINT

Ever since the 1880s, when the telephone entered the newsroom to become a fixture of modern journalism, the availability of the direct quote has made it an integral part of news writing.

A reporter with a telephone at his elbow has immediate access to persons involved in the news, as well as to those who in some way are likely to be affected by it. Thus, in every significant news story, editors look first for direct quotes from the principals. If they are not to be found, the writer will need an exceptionally convincing excuse if he is to escape the wrath of the city desk.

Why are direct quotes such a desirable feature of the modern news story? The most compelling reason is that they offer readers the maximum degree of personal contact with newsmakers obtainable in print. If in most writing the journalist functions as an intermediary between the reader and the event, by using direct quotes he is at least able to step aside and let his subjects speak for themselves.

The direct quote is especially important in stories that hinge on controversial or inflammatory statements. By providing a full quote of the statement in question, the writer protects himself from the charge that his lead is an inaccurate interpretation of the speaker's words.

Questions of accuracy aside, direct quotes also give the reader a more intimate glimpse of the subject's style and character. For this reason, they are an essential ingredient of the personality feature, and, in many instances, the dominant one.

But the reader is not the sole beneficiary of this journalistic device. The liberal use of direct quotes enables the writer to inject a considerable degree of variety into his story. Any story that is limited to a paraphrasing of the subject's remarks quickly becomes monotonous and dull. When skillfully handled, however, the interplay between paraphrase and direct quote give stories a vitality unmatched in other forms of journalistic writing.

One of the most significant effects of electronic media on print journalism during the past several decades has been the increased pressure on newsmen to approximate in their writing the immediacy of radio and television. Radio re-emphasized the spoken word and brought the living voices of world leaders into the home. Television, with its unique ability to scan the features and mannerisms of its subjects, added a whole new dimension to personal reporting. Consequently, the journalist who wishes to hold the attention of contemporary readers must flavor his writing with the personal vividness that only direct quotes and dialogue can provide.

To Quote or Not to Quote

The first problem facing beginning journalists in the handling of a subject's remarks is to decide which are to be directly quoted, which are to be paraphrased, and which are to be ignored. The basic criterion, of course, is newsworthiness, but this standard tends to be applied in different ways in different situations.

In the case of speeches, which we shall examine in greater detail later in the chapter, the news criteria must be applied rigorously if a 30-minute speech is to be reported in a half-column of type. But in a rare interview with a prominent figure, news emphasis is relaxed somewhat so that the reader can obtain a more coherent picture of the subject's views.

Once these underlying considerations have been taken into account, and a decision made as to what comments will be used, the practical problem for the writer is to decide when to quote and when to paraphrase.

We have already noted that all controversial material should be presented in direct quotes, along with preceding or following remarks if required for context. Similarly, in court reporting, all statements by witnesses relating to crucial points in a trial should be given in direct quotes.

In other kinds of stories, where controversy is not a factor, the writer uses direct quotes for remarks that express the subject's views in a particularly striking or emphatic manner.

A *New York Post* story based on comments by N.Y. Assemblyman Charles Schuler about vandalism in Brooklyn's historic Washington Cemetery, quoted Schuler as follows:

> "Vandals roam around here at will during the day and night," said Schuler. "It seems like it's become a sport in the neighborhood . . . rather than play football in the afternoon, kids come in here and kick over tombstones."

In this example, the direct quote provides a pungent summary of Schuler's view that the cemetery needed greater protection. Any attempt to paraphrase his comment would destroy its emphatic quality.

Even when a story is not built around the statements of a subject in the news, a well-chosen direct quote can heighten impact by revealing in a flash the feelings or emotional states of participants.

In the following dispatch from Reuters, a single direct quote from a kidnapping victim becomes the focal point of the story:

> MONASTEREVIN, Ireland—Dutch kidnapping victim Tiede Herrema today shouted a desperate plea for help from the house where he is held captive.
>
> "Please, let police save my life," he cried from an upstairs window at reporters clustered about 100 yards away. "They have a gun at my head."
>
> Herrema, 54, looked haggard and unshaven on his fourth day at the center of a siege around the house where Irish Republican Army guerillas are holding him prisoner . . .

Thus, as a general rule, direct quotes should be used for comments that are revelatory—comments that explain or crystallize a subject's views in a telling manner. Quotation marks accentuate whatever is contained within them, and a direct quote ought to justify that emphasis. They are not to be used for ordinary dialogue or for remarks that are obvious, repetitious or incoherent.

When it becomes necessary to include comments by a subject that are not expressed clearly or emphatically—and most colloquial speech is not—the writer turns to the paraphrase. By using this device, he can restructure or condense the material in a way that will hold the reader's interest.

In stories based on interviews, speeches or courtroom testimony, the paraphrase also serves an important transitional function. It enables the writer to change the topic smoothly and set the stage for the next direct quote, as in the following excerpt from an Associated Press story on the trial to determine the fate of Karen Anne Quinlan:

> The doctors' lawyer, Ralph Porzio, asserted that no one may order someone's death just because the quality of that life is low.
>
> "You open the gates to the deaths of thousands of people in the United States who may have a low quality of life," Porzio said. "It gives judicial sanction to the act of euthanasia," he said.
>
> Porzio acknowledged that Miss Quinlan has been given no chance of survival, but he said doctors often make mistakes in their prognoses.
>
> "If Karen Anne Quinlan has one chance in a thousand, one chance in 10 thousand, one chance in a million, who are we and by what right do we kill that chance?" he added. "Dare we defy the divine command, 'Thou shalt not kill' ?"

By skillfully using the paraphrase, the writer maintains control over his material. He can sum up statements that are rambling and obtuse in a single sentence. He can combine related ideas that are separated in the subject's own words. And he can shift the story deftly from topic to topic and from speaker to speaker.

Greater variety may be obtained in paraphrasing by occasionally using the indirect quotation. This is a form of the paraphrase that is similar to the direct quote in style, but does not use the speaker's own words. It usually appears this way:

> The present tuition rate can only be maintained, he said, by increased subsidies from the state legislature.

The indirect quotation permits the writer to come as close as possible to the speaker's own words while still allowing for some condensation and for the correction of awkward sentence structure. Indirect quotes also enable the writer to keep the speaker's remarks in their original tense.

Well-written stories based on quoted material display a subtle alternation between paraphrase and direct quote—a kind of ebb and flow—that in no small measure accounts for their unique interest and texture.

THE MECHANICS OF QUOTING

For many beginners, the most difficult part of handling direct quotes is mastering the stylistic requirements that are necessary for proper attribution. If, at first, the rules appear to be somewhat complex and arbitrary, they nevertheless will take on greater coherence as the writer becomes aware of their common objective: to leave no doubt in the reader's mind about who is speaking.

The fundamental rule of attribution, therefore, is that all statements which are not those of the writer be clearly linked to the speaker. While this may seem to be a fairly obvious requirement, many beginning writers experience considerable difficulty in determining what constitutes an adequate linkage. Much of this consternation could be avoided, I believe, if at the outset they could see that the physical paragraph is as important a factor in determining proper attribution as is the sentence. This means that while attribution is always carried out in a sentence, its ability to extend beyond that sentence is related primarily to the paragraph structure.

But let us back up a bit.

In Chapter 4 we saw how the traditional topic paragraph was broken into smaller paragraphs to improve its readability in a newspaper column. When dealing with direct quotes, the writer will find additional reasons for starting new paragraphs.

First, every new direct quote requires a new paragraph. This means that in moving from a paraphrase of the speaker's remarks to a direct quote, a new paragraph is needed, as follows:

> Commissioner Johnson predicted that an extensive police investigation of the case was about ready to produce results.
> "We have several promising leads and expect to make arrests in the next few days," he said.

It should be noted here that the preferred form for attribution in straight news writing is "he said" or "the Commissioner said" rather than "said the Commissioner," and that it should appear within or at the end of the sentence—not at the beginning. Quotation marks are placed on the outside of punctuation symbols.

If, in the above example, the writer had continued to quote Commissioner Johnson, a new paragraph would not have been needed. The quote would have taken this form:

> "We have several promising leads and expect to make arrests in the next few days," he said. "We have also received extraordinary cooperation from the business firms who were victimized by this ring."

Once a direct quote has been opened with a new paragraph, the only further paragraphing considerations are those connected with readability. A long direct quote should be indented every two or three sentences.

In handling direct quotes, the paragraph also is used to indicate a change of speaker, but a simple indentation is not a strong enough signal to alert the reader that such a shift has taken place. Thus, a new speaker is usually introduced by a paraphrase in which the speaker's name appears at the beginning as the subject of the sentence:

> Thomas Rogers, a landscape architect who appeared as a witness for the residents, testified that the proposed construction would have a detrimental effect on nearby properties.
>
> "This project," he said, "will alter the prevailing drainage patterns and more than likely cause serious erosion of adjacent land."

Transitional paragraphs of this kind are essential for clarity, especially in stories where two or more persons are quoted.

Attribution

Let us now return to the technique of attribution, which, as we noted earlier, means insuring that every direct quote is properly linked to the speaker.

The basic rule here is that every direct quote must be attributed to someone, and that attribution must appear within the first sentence of the quote. It may be placed at the end of the sentence, as in the first of the two previous examples, or it may be inserted within the sentence, as in the second example, *but it must appear in the first quoted sentence.*

Now the obvious question that follows from this rule is: how far can this first-sentence attribution be extended? To answer it, however, we will have to see the paragraph structure of a specific quote.

Having attributed a direct quote in the first sentence, we can continue the quote *in the same paragraph* without further attribution, as in the previous example:

> "We have several promising leads and expect to make arrests in the next few days," he said. "We have also received extraordinary cooperation from the business firms who were victimized by this ring."

If we are using a long direct quote, of two or more paragraphs, the first-sentence attribution can be extended indefinitely as long as one important condition is met: that the paragraph containing the attribution ends with quoted material.

Thus, the direct quotes in the above example can be extended simply by removing the quotation marks from the end of the first paragraph—to signal the reader that the quote is to continue—and by placing quotation marks at the beginning of the next paragraph, as follows:

> "We have several promising leads and expect to make arrests in the next few days," he said. "We have also received extraordinary cooperation from the business firms who were victimized by this ring.
>
> "In my ten years as police commissioner, I can't recall an investigation that elicited a comparable degree of community support."

If, on the other hand, the first paragraph should end, not with quoted material, but with attribution, the direct quote cannot be extended without new attribution in the next sentence, as in this example:

> "We have studied comparable tax programs in six other cities and our most conservative estimate is that this plan will eliminate the operating deficit in three years," the Mayor said.
>
> "We have tried to put together a tax program that would be equitable to wage earners, property owners and lower income groups," he said. "I think we have succeeded."

Paragraph structure, therefore, is the key to determining proper attribution. Recognizing this fact, writers who wish to avoid repeating "he said" or its equivalent in a long direct quote, construct their first paragraph so that the attribution does not appear at the end. One way to do this is by inserting the attribution at an appropriate break in the sentence. Another method is to conclude the paragraph with a short quoted sentence, as in the second paragraph of the previous example.

Once a running quote has been interrupted by a paraphrase, the quoted material that follows the paraphrase is subject to the same rules as the first quote; that is, it must be attributed to the speaker in the first sentence and the attribution extended according to the method described earlier.

After the second or third direct quote by the same speaker, some writers ignore the rules and present direct quotes without attribution, assuming that the reader will make the connection. But this is lazy writing. Variety is obtained by a conscious structuring of paragraphs to eliminate the need for attribution, not simply by omitting it where required.

Up to this point we have been dealing with direct quotes that are complete sentences. There are many times in the course of a story when a writer will wish to quote only words or phrases by the speaker in a sentence of his own. Here is an example:

> Councilman Greene said the tax program was "unrealistic" and that it was unlikely to produce "the exaggerated revenues projected by its designers."

Even when a partial quote ends with quoted material, as does the above example, it should *not* be extended in this manner:

> Councilman Greene said the tax program was "unrealistic" and that it was unlikely to produce "the exaggerated revenues projected by its designers. There are just too many 'ifs' in the proposal."

The correct method is to treat the partial quote as a paraphrase and to begin the continuation as a fresh quote with proper attribution, as follows:

> Councilman Greene said the tax program was "unrealistic" and that it was unlikely to produce "the exaggerated revenues projected by its designers."
>
> "There are just too many 'ifs' in the proposal," he added.

These are the essential rules for proper attribution. Their common purpose, as we noted earlier, is to enable the reader to identify the source of each quote. What can happen when they are not followed carefully by writers is shown in the following example. Taken from a story in a community weekly newspaper, this excerpt breaks almost every rule of attribution:

> Like Albert Camus, the humanist French writer-philosopher, Father Berrigan is "looking for a world in which murder will no longer be legitimate. It's too much to expect that murder won't occur at all," explained Arthur B. Jellis, the Unitarian Society's minister, introducing the Jesuit priest on March 7.
>
> "Religion often becomes a resource for the same old death game." Father Berrigan urges us to "threaten old stereotypes with new questions, shocking and uncomfortable. At times, one must be unpopular with all sides," Dr. Jellis noted.

In the first paragraph, the reader's confusion about the origin of the direct quote is compounded at the end when a new speaker is introduced. At this point the reader is uncertain whether the quote is from Albert Camus, Father Berrigan or Arthur Jellis. The second paragraph opens with an unattributed direct quote and concludes with a double-ended quote that could be attributed to either one of two possible authors.

Even readers who enjoy puzzles will be frustrated when forced to decipher a news story. By observing the rules of attribution, a writer eliminates this kind of needless confusion.

WRITING THE SPEECH STORY

Stories based on speeches, news interviews and press conferences present a real challenge to the beginning journalist since they demand a clear understanding of relative news values and story structure along with the skillful handling of direct quotes.

One of the hardest things for a beginner to grasp is that he—not the speaker—must be the ultimate judge of what is newsworthy. A young reporter sent out to cover a speech by a prominent public official is likely to be overawed by his subject. If he is not careful, the reporter will find himself accepting the speaker's values as his own.

The reporter must understand that he is covering the event as a representative of the newspaper's readers, and that comments made by the speaker must be judged on the basis of their relevance to this group rather than the audience, which already has expressed a special interest by attending. This means that the reporter is free to disregard the speaker's order altogether and to use material that he believes is of interest to the reader in a way that reflects its relative importance.

There are many times when remarks made by a speaker during a question-and-answer period following a speech turn out to be more newsworthy than anything said in the prepared address. When this is the case, the reporter should have no qualms about building his lead on this material.

The reporter's purpose in covering a speech, as in any other event, is to look for *news*. It is not simply to produce a summary of the speaker's remarks. Political candidates may give the same speech over and over again during the course of a campaign, but reporters who continue to write stories based on these remarks insult the intelligence of their readers.

By refusing to pass on comments by candidates that are repetitious, irrelevant or frivolous, reporters can help to raise the level of political discourse. If such standards were to be applied generally by the press, candidates would learn quickly that in order to see their words in print, they must address the issues with intelligence and imagination.

In most speech reporting, however, the writer does not have to maintain as rigorous a criterion for newsworthiness. Reporters often are sent out to cover speeches that are not expected to produce any significant news. In these cases, factors other than the speech itself may affect news values, such as the appearance of a prominent national figure in the newspaper's area or retirement ceremonies for a well-known local official.

Even here the reporter should be on the lookout for the most interesting or unusual remarks, or audience response that might give his account a touch of color. A reporter is never released from his obligation to look for news—not even when the odds are against finding it.

The Advance Text

The effort involved in writing the speech story has been lessened somewhat in recent years by the almost universal practice of speakers to provide the press with an advance copy of their remarks.

A writer who has a neatly mimeographed copy of a speech next to his typewriter can prepare a story with a minimum of time and effort. He can quickly leaf through the pages with a red pencil in hand, marking passages that are particularly newsworthy or striking. By the time he has scanned the whole text, a lead is likely to suggest itself, and he then can build his story with direct quotes that leave no nagging doubts about their accuracy.

But he must also be aware of the limitations of the advance text. A mimeographed speech gives no indication of the vocal or gestural emphasis that a speaker may add to certain remarks. Nor is it any guarantee of what the speaker ultimately will say. Encouraged by a responsive audience, speakers have been known to interject comments far more newsworthy than anything contained in the prepared text.

Thus, if the speech is an important one by a major speaker, the writer should plan to attend, even though he may have an advance text. He then can follow the prepared remarks as the subject speaks, noting any changes or additions. By doing so, the writer spares his paper the embarrassment of missing significant news.

Newspapers with deadlines that come before the time of the speech can write their story based on the advance text, but they should protect themselves by including the phrase, "in a speech prepared for delivery . . ." This notifies the reader that the story was written prior to the actual delivery of the address.

Note Taking

To cover speeches effectively without an advance text, the writer must acquire some degree of skill in taking notes. Yet skillful note taking—at least from a journalistic point of view—is more than simple stenography. Formal systems of shorthand may be helpful, but sooner or later every writer develops his own method of abbreviated notation. The single most important aspect of taking good notes is the ability to listen critically to what the speaker is saying.

The writer who remains alert to the substance of the speaker's remarks and takes notes only when they are newsworthy will find, when he begins to write his story, that half the work already has been done. His notes will be a digest of the major points of the speech, and his only task will be to construct a lead and develop an orderly story from them. If, on the other hand, he has functioned mainly as a stenographer, taking down comments without discretion, he will be faced with the time-consuming job of reviewing all of his notes and sorting out what is important before he can even begin to write.

Good writers do not waste time or energy. They listen for the significant comment or the telling phrase and then take notes. By eliminating trite or irrelevant material at this stage, they are ready to write when they return to their typewriters. Writers who have trained themselves to listen perceptively will be surprised to discover how much more easily they are able to remember the speaker's ideas without the aid of notes.

Notes that are most useful to a writer are a skeletonized form of the ideas and comments he wishes to record. Consisting mainly of key words and phrases, with articles and prepositions omitted in the interest of speed, these fragments can be reconstituted into complete thoughts as the writer begins his story. When he wishes to quote his subject, the writer uses quotation marks in his notes and takes down the statement as accurately as possible.

Note taking and the reporting of speeches are skills that must be learned by practice. We have emphasized certain aspects of the technique here only because they are inseparably linked to the production of an accurate and coherent story.

Speech Story Structure

In writing a story based on a speech, the journalist's objective is the same as in writing any other type of story, that is, to focus on the news. Hence, the leads of most speech stories consist of a statement summarizing either the overall theme, if that is newsworthy, or a section of the speech that is particularly significant.

In either case, the lead reflects what the writer feels is the most important aspect of the speech. One of the most common mistakes made by beginners in handling a speech story is to ignore the speaker's remarks altogether and build a lead on the circumstances of the speech, as in this example:

> John R. Busbee, a public opinion analyst, was the speaker last night at the annual membership meeting of the League of Women Voters of Greensburg.

This lead is unacceptable simply because it contains no news; in fact, it could have been written the day before the event. In a speech story, the news is what the speaker said, and if he said nothing worth reporting, no story should be written.

Once the writer has singled out the material for his lead, his task is to cast it in a form that is both clear and emphatic. With few exceptions, the most effective way to do this is by paraphrasing the speaker.

It is always a temptation for writers to let the speaker write their lead for them by using a direct quote. But while it requires less effort on the part of the writer, the result is often neither clear nor emphatic. It normally takes this form:

> "Fewer and fewer voters between the ages of 18 and 26 claim any allegiance to the two major political parties, or any party for that matter."
>
> This is the finding of John R. Busbee, a public opinion analyst who last night addressed the annual membership meeting of the League of Women Voters of Greensburg.

We can assume that the above lead contains the angle that the writer wishes to emphasize. We must be aware, however, that it was written to be part of a whole speech and that it may not measure up to the more stringent requirements for a good news lead. If it does not, the fault lies, not with the speaker, but with the writer who used it as his lead.

In any given address, the speaker's most interesting point may not be found in a single quotation. It might be what is implied by a series of remarks, or by the speech as a whole. The specific task of the writer is to bring these ideas together for the reader. Thus, in the above example, a more enterprising writer might have written:

> A public opinion analyst has predicted that the growing sense of alienation among younger voters from established political parties will be a significant factor in electoral politics in the next decade.
>
> In a speech last night to the League of Women Voters of Greensburg, John R. Busbee, a research analyst with Public Opinion Research Associates, said studies conducted by his firm during the past three years have shown a dramatic decline in party affiliation among voters in the 18 to 26 age group.
>
> "Prospective candidates who ignore these trends," he added, "will have little chance of success at the polls."
>
> Busbee also pointed out that . . .

The speech story begins, therefore, with the most newsworthy aspect of the speech as summarized by the writer. If the speaker used unusually strong or colorful language to express these views, the writer may elect to quote certain words or phrases, as in the following lead from the *Boston Globe:*

> WASHINGTON—President Ford will try to beat back Ronald Reagan's suddenly-strong bid for the GOP presidential nomination by having supporters portray Reagan as a man who would risk war through "unreasonable bellicosity," a campaign spokesman said yesterday.

Once he has stated the main news angle in the lead, the writer can begin an elaboration of this idea with paraphrase and direct quotes. If he feels, however, that the speech contained other remarks approaching the lead in importance, he may wish to summarize these in the second paragraph before elaborating the lead. In overall development, the speech story follows the basic pattern of the inverted pyramid, with the most important remarks preceding the least important in a subtle interplay of paraphrase and direct quotation.

In the following example from the *New York Times* of April 5, 1968, events and actions surrounding a speech became an integral part of an unusually colorful story:

> BERKELEY, Calif., April 4—Senator Eugene J. McCarthy disarmed hostile "New Leftists" in a crowd of 10,000 students at the University of California today by proposing amnesty for draft dodgers who fled to Canada.
>
> The Minnesota Senator also promised, if elected President, to curb the power of the Central Intelligence Agency, the Federal Bureau of Investigation and the Selective Service System.
>
> Starting his drive to win California's Presidential primary June 4, the Senator took his campaign to the place where the New Left started its campus revolt four years ago.
>
> His incursion seemed at first to court disaster. Earlier in the day the campus was the scene of a rally sponsored by the New Left Forum at which literature denouncing Senator McCarthy as a member of the "establishment" was distributed.
>
> Hundreds of New Leftists carrying signs demanding immediate withdrawal from Vietnam, then flocked to Greek Theater and awaited the Senator. They occupied strategic spots around the ampitheater, a few climbing the eucalyptus trees in the rear, and their hoots almost equalled the applause when the Senator appeared.
>
> Campus dogs of all breeds and sizes raced up and down the aisles contributing to the clamor.
>
> At a signal the New Leaftists raised their banners— placards of black lettering on shocking pink that gave the arena a psychedelic air.
>
> Soon the hecklers were in full cry.
>
> "Some said I was a Judas goat trying to lead the people back to President Johnson," Senator McCarthy said.

"Right," cried the New Leftists.

"Some said I was a stalking horse for Senator Kennedy," the Senator added.

"Right," chorused the hecklers.

"Right?" asked the Senator in mock bewilderment. "Pretty hard to do both, I'll tell you."

Laughter and applause drowned out the hecklers and for the rest of his speech Senator McCarthy had the crowd with him.

He drew his biggest applause when he said he favored cutting the power of three agencies that had become, he said, independent sources of "decision and power—the C.I.A., the F.B.I. and the draft board under General Hershey."

He said he favored a "kind of amnesty" for draft evaders who had gone to Canada.

He said he would offer the young men amnesty if they agreed to alternative service either in military or civilian life, and he would offer the same to any draft objectors in this country.

Earlier, arriving at the San Francisco airport, he was asked about rumors that Richard M. Goodwin, a former speech writer for Presidents Kennedy and Johnson, might be preparing to leave his organization.

"As far as I know he's still with me," Senator McCarthy said. "And as far as I know he's still likely to remain. He's a kind of a professional. I mean he can pitch for either the Cards or the Braves and move from one to the other in mid-season without giving away any signals."

The Democratic National Committeewoman from California, Mrs. Ann Alanson gave her endorsement to Senator Kennedy this morning. National Committeeman Eugene Wyman is still with the "loyalty slate" committed to President Johnson.

In this story, the veteran *New York Times* reporter Homer Bigart deftly weaves together McCarthy's remarks and the comments and behavior of the audience. Had he restricted his account to the words of the speaker, he would have given readers an incomplete and lifeless picture of the event.

7 : VARIETIES OF THE BASIC STRUCTURE

Apart from its importance as a method of organizing the news, the "inverted pyramid" has served the craft of journalism as a discipline for training writers to extract the essential elements from a given mass of facts.

So valuable is this skill to the journalist that the inverted pyramid could conceivably be retained as a training device long after its function in organizing the news has ceased.

Already, many prominent figures in journalism are predicting the gradual demise of the inverted pyramid form. But even those who are more cautious must admit that it no longer occupies the commanding position that it once held in the writing of news.

Stories that in the early 1960s would have been written in strict inverted pyramid style are appearing today in a variety of forms. Even the wire services—the agencies most responsible for the development of the inverted pyramid—are experimenting with news structure.

The following example was taken from the United Press International wire:

> MONTPELIER—For more than five years, Paul D. Lawrence fashioned a reputation as a supercop, a one-man crusader against drug dealers, whose undercover work and testimony led to hundreds of arrests and convictions.
>
> Local police—often short-handed, ill-trained and under community pressure to stamp out drug abuse—eagerly sought his services from the St. Albans Police Department, where he was an undercover narcotics officer.

> Then, on July 12, 1974, Lawrence was arrested and charged with eight counts of perjury and obtaining policy money under false pretenses. He was later convicted on several counts.
>
> Calling it ''a very sad day for Vermont law enforcement,'' Gov. Thomas Salmon yesterday announced he will grant ''complete and unconditional'' pardons to persons convicted because of Lawrence's uncorroborated testimony.
>
> Salmon released a report . . .

Had a UPI staffer handed in such a story a decade earlier, it would have been bounced back with a curt reminder to put the news in the lead. Obviously, something is happening to the structure of the news.

What is happening, of course, is that the full effects of the electronic revolution are now being felt throughout print media. One of the effects is the stress on originality and variety in news presentation, and it can be seen structurally in the emergence of new weekly newspapers marked by vigorous writing and attractive graphic design. Within the established dailies, this effect takes the form of simplified layout and a relaxation of the inverted pyramid style.

When print was the dominant news medium, writers used other news styles, among them the sequential story which followed chronology or the suspended interest story built on climactic order, but they usually were reserved for human interest material outside the mainstream of the news. Today, however, stylistic innovation and variety are an integral part of news writing.

As television and radio become increasingly dominant in spot news coverage, print media are beginning to experiment with new forms for the more comprehensive reporting that is now expected of them. Those who are planning to enter print journalism in the electronic age should be aware that the skills demanded of today's writers will go well beyond a simple mastery of the inverted pyramid style, important as that is.

The inverted pyramid is an extremely useful organizing

technique as long as the writer is focusing on the "today" aspect of the news. It is only when he begins to lengthen his perspective and search for meaning and significance that the inverted pyramid becomes overly rigid and mechanical. At this point the writer must create a structure that is organically related to his material.

In the following *Washington Post* story, a writer attempts to explain a series of actions occuring over a period of months. Since there is no "today" angle, he must modify the inverted pyramid to accommodate a wider news perspective:

> WASHINGTON—In the last two months, senior members of the Ford Administration have quietly stripped Agriculture Secretary Butz of much of his power to formulate food policy and make grain export decisions on his own.
>
> As a result, some senior Agriculture Dept. officials are angry. They say that foreign agriculture policy is influenced more and more by "instant experts" at the White House or "striped pants" diplomats at the State Dept.
>
> Top officials at other agencies confirm that the Argiculture Dept. has been required to share its decision-making power and add that the power shift is necessary because of the large impact that food policy can have on prices at home and diplomacy abroad.
>
> "Defense policy is too important to be left to the generals and agricultural policy is too important to be left to the Dept. of Agriculture," said an official this week. . .

Despite considerable experimentation, the inverted pyramid continues to be the most conspicuous news form in the daily press. A daily newspaper must justify the frequency of its publication or readers might suspect that they don't have to read it every day. It does this by giving the bulk of its news a "today" angle, that is, by making most stories appear to be important links in a chain of events.

Weekly newspapers, by definition, are relieved of this preoccupation with "today" and thus have greater freedom to explore the wider implications of the news. It is in this area of print media, especially in the new weeklies that have appeared since the coming of television, that the widest variety of writing styles can be observed.

Except for the fully developed feature article, the older alternative forms common to the daily press consisted of short human interest items that served as a contrast to the more formal and impersonal presentation of "hard news." Today's new forms are an attempt to make the hard news itself more meaningful and interesting to read.

THE TRADITIONAL ALTERNATIVES

When radio emerged as a dynamic new medium during the 1920s, it created a demand in the daily press for short human interest items to brighten news columns that by comparison were sober and monotonous. Since this material was rarely obtainable in sufficient quantity at the local level, the wire services moved quickly into the field.

Sensing a potential market for the well-written human interest story, both the Associated Press and United Press urged their respective bureaus to be on the lookout for unusual material. Such stories in rough form would be sent to New York where staff members with a flair for this kind of copy rewrote them for the national wires.

From the 1930s on—except for those periods when war news and casualty lists filled all available news space—human interest items from the wires could be found scattered throughout American daily newspapers. In these stories, the inverted pyramid was cast aside and the information was structured to fit the story.

Here is an example from Associated Press in 1930:

> YONKERS, N.Y., Nov. 23 (A.P.)—The executive type stick-up man went to work (with a gun) in a restaurant early today. He issued orders to the manager, George Van Sork.
>
> "Put down that milk," he commanded. Van Sork did, without a word.

"Get over that counter." Van Sork did, saying nothing.

"Shove those dishes back." It was done without comment.

"Give me your money." It was $22.40, and Van Sork handed it over, still without a word.

The stick-up man backed toward the door.

"Don't move," he ordered, "until you hear my motor start.

"And," he added, "the next time you're held up don't talk so much."

If the writing style of many of these early stories seems primitive by comparison to later examples, the writers nevertheless were establishing structural patterns that would persist for the next four decades. They leaned heavily on the narrative, suspended interest and dialogue. And they strove for clever, unconventional leads that would excite the reader's curiosity, as in this example from the United Press in 1953:

TOKYO, Nov. 21 (UP)—Japanese railroad engineers want a raise in pay so badly that they just have to let off a little steam.

They decided to do it all together at noon next Wednesday. They will blow the whistles of 5,000 locomotives for one full minute.

The engineers chapter of the National Railway Workers Union said this will cost the government, which operates the railroads, 130 yen (about 30 cents) per engine, or the equivalent of $1,500.

An Associated Press story from the same year is a classic example of the suspended interest technique:

SOUTH BEND, Ind., Nov. 25 (AP)—When Paul Hayn left home this morning to take his wife to the maternity ward in Osteopathic Hospital he thought he knew where the hospital was.

He drove 25 miles from Walkerton, southwest of South Bend, through the south side section where the hospital is and pulled up in front of the Mar-Main Arms apartment on the far north side. He escorted his wife into the ornate lobby before he discovered his error. Then it was too late to get back to the hospital.

His wife, Dorothy, 25, gave birth to a daughter in the apartment house lobby. The mother and baby were taken in a police car to near-by Memorial Hospital where both were reported in good condition.

The wire service human interest shorts became the models for alternative structure, and newsmen across the country copied the styles whenever an opportunity presented itself. The opportunities must have been rare. Except for stylistic experiments in a handful of tabloids, there were relatively few attempts by daily newspapers prior to the 1960s to apply imaginative writing techniques to the news.

Full-length features during this time usually were devoted to interesting personalities and places well outside the mainstream of the news. The news features that did appear, prior to World War II, were with few exceptions "sidebars" that accompanied a straight news story about the same event.

The following story from the *Philadelphia Inquirer* is fairly typical of the sidebar feature. It appeared in conjunction with several news stories about Wendell Willkie's triumphal visit to Philadelphia during the 1940 presidential election campaign:

With that peculiar talent for getting the neck in the noose that some people have, Ezra Kirby went out yesterday and bought himself a dozen eggs.

Ordinarily this is considered a harmless thing to do, and many people do it year after year without incurring anything worse than stains on the vest.

However, Kirby also decided, in a rash moment on his way to his home at 180 Manheim st., Germantown, to stop in at the Wendell Willkie rally at Shibe Park.

Kirby is one of those mild-mannered, gray-haired people of the type always being thrown into the jail house while ferocious-looking types go unmolested, so as soon as Detective Henry Dermody, of the anti-egg squad, spotted him heading for the ring-side seats, he stepped up.

"What've you got there, brother?" he inquired.

"Eggs," said Kirby.

"Ah—eggs!" snorted Detective Dermody, "Eggs, huh?"

"Yes—eggs," replied Kirby innocently.

"Place this character in the wagon, men," commanded Detective Dermody, "He has got eggs."

Now all this was very puzzling to Kirby, who did not know (A) that anybody with eggs at a Willkie meeting is automatically a suspicious character since the recent hurling of such missiles at the Republican candidate in Michigan; (B) that a whole squad of detectives had been assigned to guard against similar occurrences at the Shibe Park meeting; and (C) that just a few moments before he arrived an egg had been hurled at Willkie's car from a seat in the upper tier in spite of the vigilance of this mob of constabulary.

So they carted Kirby away to the outskirts of the ball park, where he made things twice as bad for himself by announcing that he was from some place near Elwood, Ind., Willkie's home town. That clinched it. He was taken to City Hall station at once.

He was questioned and requestioned, cross-examined and stripped of everything but the big Willkie button he was wearing—but he stoutly maintained he hadn't meant any harm, that he just dropped in because Willkie was a home-town boy, and that he had bought the eggs strictly for eating purposes.

At a late hour last night, he finally was released, a much bewildered man. He added one interesting note in his conversation with detectives.

"I'm one former resident of Elwood who never knew Willkie as a boy," he confided.

The above story has almost no significance as straight news. Its appeal lies solely in the strong human interest aspect that permits the reader to identify closely with the plight of Ezra Kirby. Sensing the potential of this small incident to provide a humorous sidelight to the straight reporting of a major political event, the writer wisely has structured his story in a manner that enhances its essential appeal. In this case it is a simple chronology coupled with interesting dialogue and perceptive comments by the writer.

As we noted in Chapter 2, it was World War II and the complex events leading up to it that gave foreign correspondents a unique opportunity for interpretative reporting. There were many times when a reporter at the front line had to move beyond a simple recounting of information and, as an eyewitness, make a judgment on the overall situation. On these occasions, correspondents set aside the inverted pyramid and began the story with a summary of their own analysis, as did the writer of the following example from the *New York Times* in 1943:

> ON THE TUNISIAN FRONT, Feb. 14—Reichsfuehrer Hitler cannot afford to lose one battle in Tunisia. So narrow is the eastern seacoast corridor that the Germans hold between Field Marshal General Erwin Rommel's position south of the Mareth line and the Tunis-Bizerte area that the loss of one battle would split the German forces.
>
> Despite this and the Russian defeats, Herr Hitler is rushing infantry by planes and ships from Europe and it is obvious to those on the spot that this North African campaign is becoming a showdown rather than a sideshow in the preparation for the attack on Europe. To win, Herr Hitler's forces—under Marshal Rommel, Col. Gen Dietloff von Arnim acting as a local commander in the north—must, by one device or another, get more elbow room by cracking through the line of mountains nearest the sea.
>
> This correspondent in the past twenty-four hours has travelled from Medjez-el-Bab, our position nearest Tunis, to Gafsa, an oasis on the British First Army's southern flank. On both sides patrol activities are grimmer . . .

The result, as the above example indicates, is a story that provides real insight into the news. From the standpoint of meaning, one story like this is worth any number of fragmentary accounts listing troop movements, casualties, equipment losses, etc.

Although sporadic efforts were made after the war to apply these techniques to public affairs reporting at home, the real impetus for experimentation was yet to come.

THE NEW ALTERNATIVES

If the dynamism of radio had forced newspapers to reexamine news content and sharpen writing style, the coming of television in the late 1940s would have even more profound effects on print journalism. This new medium had the unique ability to place the viewer at the center of the news event by providing him with aural, visual and—according to at least one observer— even tactile perception of its subjects.

The television image, in the view of Marshall McLuhan, "requires each instant that we 'close' the spaces in the mesh by a convulsive sensuous participation that is profoundly kinetic and tactile, because tactility is the interplay of the senses, rather than the isolated contact of skin and object."

However we may explain the nature of this experience, one fact seems indisputably clear: when compared to the rich sensory involvement offered by the TV image, the traditional newspaper page, both in form and content, appears to be static and superficial.

It is this fact more than any other that accounts for the dramatic changes in print media that have occurred since the early 1960s. The most interesting experiments in format and writing style have taken place within the "new media"—the "underground" press of the '60s and the new weeklies and city magazines of the '70s—but even the daily press has been forced by television to improve its content and graphics.

In an attempt to create a more dynamic format, daily newspapers reduced the number of columns from eight to six and switched to "horizontal" make-up systems that utilized fewer stories on a page. These efforts went hand-in-hand with increased concern for photographic display and a more sophisticated handling of type faces. Added incentive for brightening the newspaper image came from the mechanical side where rapid advances in printing technology were outstripping the ability of the press to use them effectively.

One result of the renovation in graphics was a sharp reduction in the number of three- and four-paragraph stories that once cluttered newspaper pages. Short human interest items now were gathered together and run in special columns under a standing head. This contributed to an overall design that called for a relatively few strong elements on each page.

Conversely, longer stories were needed to run in horizontal blocks under multi-column headlines. Thus, the requirements of the "new graphics" served only to reinforce the growing demand for in-depth reporting—another TV by-product. As we have already noted, the inverted pyramid continues to be the predominant news structure in the daily press. Nevertheless, today's newspapers are allocating more space than ever to interpretative news features, investigative articles and to experimentation with journalistic forms.

An indication of the shift in daily newspaper values is the appearance on front pages—traditionally a sacrosanct area for only the most significant hard news—of features and decorative photographic displays. On May 6, 1976, the *Boston Globe* devoted the top of its front page to a feature on the changing nature of volunteer workers—a story that at one time would have been relegated to the women's section. Two weeks later, the *Washington Post* used five full columns above the fold for a feature story and picture related to the reopening of Ellis Island in New York harbor as a national monument.

The daily press has responded to the dynamism of electronic media by ending the strict segregation of news and features, by giving writers greater leeway in the areas of interpretative reporting and stylistic innovation, and by striving to upgrade its graphic quality. This has resulted in a newspaper that, while providing essential information, offers readers a more stimulating and visually satisfying experience.

If television has had a considerable impact on daily newspapers—even to the point of eliminating many of them—its most significant effect in the print area has been the fostering of a whole new category of media: the new urban and regional weekly newspapers. All of the most prominent examples of this new journalistic form have appeared in the wake of television broadcasting, and all reflect to some degree the altered media relationships brought about by electronic journalism.

The new newspapers begin by accepting television and radio as the dominant news media of our time. They recognize that the very structure of electronic media lends itself to the instantaneous processing of national and international news, rather than that which is local and regional. Even in urban areas, a major portion of local television news consists of material that can be gathered readily from a few central points, such as municipal government, police, or business and labor sources.

Rather than compete with electronic media, as many dailies have attempted to do, the new weeklies have been established expressly to complement the news gathering functions of television and radio. Thus, they concentrate almost exclusively on in-depth reporting of the local or regional scene. Since they are not burdened with the added responsibility of carrying national and international news, these publications are free to develop a format and writing style that is appropriate to their unique purpose.

As a result, the new weeklies have led the way in adapting the most recent technological advances in the graphic arts to newspaper design and production. All, without exception, have chosen a tabloid format, which permits a simpler and more dramatic page layout built around a single pictorial or typographic element. All are produced by one of several "cold" typesetting methods combined with offset printing. All have chosen type faces that express a strongly contemporary mood, and many make use of a second or third color to add impact to the nameplate and standing heads.

As weeklies, these newspapers have no need to incorporate a "today" angle in their stories, and, accordingly, the straight inverted pyramid structure is rarely used, except for brief items that have not been reported in the daily press. Long investigative articles and shorter topical stories are structured as features, with the lead focused on a significant or provocative aspect of the story rather than on a single action in a narrow time frame.

Even when the story relates directly to an event that has taken place in the week prior to publication, the writer attempts to place the lead in a wider context, as in the following example from the weekly *Pacific Sun* of Marin County, California:

> While recommending drastic job cuts in other county departments, County Administrator John Barrows is asking an increase in his own. The anomaly surfaced Tuesday when the proposed $55,155,000 county budget for fiscal '75–'76 was presented to the Board of Supervisors.
>
> Barrows' office is now staffed by seven employees and his budget request calls for 8.5—the addition of a deputy county administrator, at $2200 a month, and a half time aide.
>
> The most severely injured department . . .

The result is a more meaningful lead and a story that loses none of its importance by appearing several days after the event.

In some instances, the weeklies simply ignore the "when" aspect altogether, as did the *San Francisco Bay Guardian* in this story:

> Taxi Unlimited, an independent cab company in Berkeley, has had a head-on collision with the landlord who owns Taxi's office building
>
> The landlord, Mark Hajjar, wants Taxi out so he can convert the building he bought last December into a complex of small shops. Taxi, which is organized as a collective, says it can't afford to move and claims the company may fold if evicted.
>
> Taxi hopes to pressure Hajjar into letting the company stay in its present location (1908 Berkeley Way at Grove St.) by mobilizing public opinion against him.
>
> So far Taxi's campaign . . .

In longer articles, the new weeklies use all of the feature writer's techniques: arresting leads, organic structure, forceful imagery, interesting dialogue and strong endings. First-person stories are common and interviews often take the form of question and answer reportage.

Since we shall discuss feature writing techniques at length in Chapter 9, there is no need to describe them here. The following excerpt from an investigative article in the *Boston Phoenix* illustrates how these techniques can be utilized to draw a reader into the story:

> The land was, of course, all theirs in the beginning, before an English explorer named their island Martha's Vineyard for his daughter.
>
> Now the Gay Head Indians, a branch of the nearly extinct Wampanoag tribe which met the Pilgrims 355 years ago, want some of it back. They claim 230 acres they consider tribal lands that were taken illegally over a hundred years ago, when the Indian district at the western tip of Martha's Vineyard was incorporated into a town. These lands include the famous clay cliffs of Gay Head—one of the island's biggest tourist attractions—Herring Creek, and a large tract of wild cranberry bogs.
>
> That they want the land back is not at all surprising. The astonishing thing is that the Indians actually have a chance of recovering it from the present owner, the town of Gay Head. Unlike their Western cousins, this tribe has more than a moral claim; it might have a solid legal claim to title as well. Three weeks ago, the Wampanoag Tribal Council of Gay Head won the first round of the fight to regain title when Federal District Court Judge W. Arthur Garrity refused to dismiss their suit as the town had requested . . .

When news can be presented with grace and understanding, as in the above example, it loses its fragmentary character and becomes for the reader a rewarding and meaningful source of information.

8 : THE NEWS
IN CONTEXT

Jacques Ellul, the noted French social historian, has raised disturbing questions about the proliferation of news by mass media and its effect on the ability of citizens and their leaders to make sound political decisions.

In his book, *The Political Illusion,* a provocative study of contemporary political institutions, Ellul goes so far as to declare that "the predominance of news produces a fundamental political incapacity in the individual." This incapacity, according to Ellul, is brought on by an overdose of diverse and discontinuous information. "In order not to drown in this incessant flow," he adds, "man is forced to forget."

And it is this forgetting that has profound significance in the realm of politics, as Ellul points out:

> There is no politics where there is no grasp of the past, where there is no continuity, where there is no analysis of errors or capacity to understand the present through that analysis and in that continuity. But current events obscure everything, even for the specialists. Current news pre-empts the sense of continuity, prevents the use of memory, and leads to a constant falsification of past events when they are evoked again in the stream of news.

Ellul's comments may come as a shock to many journalists who, like their readers, have accepted without question the conventional wisdom of our society that has made a virtue of "being well-informed." While such emphasis on information may help to sell news media, it nevertheless blurs the critical distinction between the simple amassing of factual data and *understanding,* which is the ability to relate facts in some meaningful way.

104

This distinction was never more tragically illustrated than during the recent war in Vietnam. On one side were the optimistic reports of Pentagon officials who were counting on the superiority of their computerized information systems to bring the conflict to a desired conclusion. On the other, were the ominous but ultimately prophetic stories by journalists like David Halberstam and the late Bernard Fall who looked beyond day-to-day events and placed the war within the context of Vietnamese history and culture.

Turning specifically to electronic media, Professor Ellul notes that television has served only to heighten the emphasis on immediacy in contemporary political affairs:

> Is it not exciting to participate personally via TV in the birth of a great political decision; and is it not a matter of great import to see directly all these great personages agitated over such great problems? Such problems are evidently the most interesting; the limelight of the news illumines them, dramatizes and exalts them, and digs up each of their details.

But he adds:

> These are false political problems because they are always appearances only, visible consequences, manifestations of deeper and more decisive problems from which the citizen living in the news turns away because they are not as exciting as the latest speech.

In this sense, electronic media have become captives of the news, for until a problem has taken visible form as an event or spectacle, it cannot be videotaped. Hence, in the electronic age, the primary responsibility for putting the news into a meaningful framework falls upon the print journalist.

Of all media, it is the printed word that is best suited to making the public aware of the decisive currents that run well below the agitated surface of events. And only in print can the relevant past be combined with present data to suggest a feasible future.

To keep Ellul's "citizen living in the news" from turning

away from the important but non-spectacular message, the print journalist will need to muster every skill at his command—certainly in writing, but also in typography and graphic design. How effectively he meets this challenge may well determine the future of democratic political life.

Mary McCarthy saw clearly the unique role of print media in her book, *The Mask of State: Watergate Portraits:*

> Printer's ink and domestic liberty have an old association. Whereas television, being a mass medium, can be controlled and manipulated, total control of the printed word, as has been demonstrated in the Soviet Union, seems to be all but impossible. If newspapers are censored or suppressed, broadsides and leaflets can still circulate, passing from hand to hand.

It might appear from all of the above that the job of putting the news in context is reserved for a rather select group of writers who are charged with analyzing national or foreign affairs. Nothing could be farther from the truth. The task of piecing together those fragments that are the substance of current news falls on every journalist in every area of reporting.

Let us look now at some basic techniques that can be used to make news more meaningful.

PUTTING THE NEWS TOGETHER

The simplest and most fundamental relationship that can exist between two news items is that both are parts of a larger story.

This relationship can be readily observed in sequential stories about a continuing event, such as a major criminal trial. But it is present whenever a story relates to some prior news event, regardless of the span of time intervening. It is the journalist's duty to discover such relationships and make them clear to the reader.

To illustrate problems of identification in Chapter 3, we

used the example of a boy who died from injuries received two weeks earlier in a playground accident. The accident itself, in which a boy was critically injured, was a news story. And the death of an eight-year-old boy also is news, if only an obituary. But the second story has no real meaning to the reader unless it is related to the first.

In the above example, the connection between the stories is hard to miss. The real challenge to the journalist, however, is the relationship that is not obvious and which must be uncovered with some effort. Here there are no set rules, only the basic admonition to be always on the lookout.

Success in establishing important but hidden relationships comes most often to journalists who are willing to invest time and energy in the process. Undoubtedly the major success story of our time is that of Carl Bernstein and Bob Woodward, the *Washington Post* reporters whose dogged persistence in running down leads ultimately produced the Watergate revelations.

Few journalists, of course, will have an opportunity to unearth a story of this magnitude. Yet every story that suggests a relationship to other events should be checked out with the basic research tools of the journalist: clipping files, public records and interviews. Not to follow through when a relationship is suggested makes the writer a perpetrator of the kind of discontinuity that Professor Ellul finds so debilitating to political life.

Having established a connection between events, the next task is to express it clearly for the reader. Where there is a simple relationship to an earlier story, the linkage—or ''tieback'' as it is called in the newsroom—should be spelled out in the lead, as in this example from the *Boston Globe:*

> TEWKSBURY—Police yesterday, without disclosing any details, said they have questioned three suspects in the New Year's Eve slayings of a prominent Tewksbury gynecologist, his wife and son. The three persons have not been held.

In the case of the ''running story''—the story that appears daily about a continuing news event, the tie-back becomes progressively briefer and may eventually drop into the second or third paragraph. The assumption here is that the reader has seen some of the preceding accounts.

News writers, however, cannot assume too much about the reader's prior knowledge. Except for continuing stories of major significance, the writer must include enough material from earlier accounts to make the story completely understandable to first-time readers. These are the readers to whom the news writer must address himself, and they are the norm by which effective writing is measured.

Thus, in every story about a continuing event, there must be a recapitulation of what has occurred prior to the immediate account. This enables readers who have not seen earlier stories to make sense of the latest one. The recapitulation may require several paragraphs, but as the event progresses, earlier material is condensed sharply to make room for more recent background information.

In the following story from the *Philadelphia Inquirer,* the writer must bridge a gap of more than a year between the original story and the follow-up. He does this effectively by providing an immediate tie-back in the lead and then, after reporting on the latest development, by recapitulating the events preceding it.

For emphasis, we have italicized the recapitulation in this example:

> A Common Pleas Court judge yesterday ordered the City of Philadelphia to fire 380 laborers who received preferential treatment in an 8,000-man job competition in September 1974
>
> Judge Maurice W. Sporkin ordered the city to dismiss the workers from the streets and water departments within 30 days.
>
> During that 30-day period, the judge ruled, the city is free to determine a procedure to hire replacements for the 380 workers.
>
> If the city does not come up with a new procedure within the 30 days, it will be required to hire new laborers from an

eligibility list previously drawn up by the American Arbitration Association.

Judge Sporkin's ruling climaxed a protracted and complex legal battle that lasted almost a year and a half.

The case involves three parties: the city, District Council 33 of the American Federation of State, County and Municipal Employes Union (AF-SCME), and a court-appointed trustee, David H. Marion, who represents the 8,000 men who failed to get city jobs.

The controversy began on Sept. 7, 1974, a rainy Saturday, after the city had advertised that it was going to award 700 Civil Service jobs for laborers on a first-come, first-served basis.

About 8,000 hopeful job seekers lined up that day to apply for the openings.

Unknown to them, more than half the openings had already been awarded to provisional city employes. The provisionals had been hired through a variety of political, union and administrative influences.

Those workers had been told—many of them by letter—that if they wanted permanent jobs they should arrive 10 to 12 hours before the publicly announced starting time for applying at seven recreation centers.

The recreation centers were opened five or six hours early, virtually assuring that the provisionals would get the jobs.

The whole matter was taken to court that fall when District Council 33 filed a suit seeking to protect the provisionals.

City Personnel Director Lewis S. Taylor, who said he had not yet seen Judge Sporkin's order would not comment.

Taylor said that it was his "intention to use the lottery (eligibility) list" in selecting replacements for the laborers. However, he said he could not be sure of the final selection procedure since department heads also have discretion in the method of appointment.

In follow-up stories where the background information is not as lengthy as in the above account, the writer may choose to weave it into the new material and avoid breaking the flow of the news.

Putting the News in Context

We have seen in the previous section how a news story can lack meaning when not firmly linked to prior events to which it is essentially related. There are other ways, however, in which news can be rendered meaningless. Even stories that have no relation to previous news events can be without meaning for the reader if the writer fails to provide information that, while not a part of the immediate story, is necessary for its understanding.

Such information is essential for reporting the activities of public bodies like city councils or school boards. For a reporter to write that a proposed ordinance has been referred to a particular committee is meaningless. Every city hall reporter soon learns that one committee may mean sudden death for a bill while another may speed its passage. Unless he shares this information with the reader, his story is incomplete.

All complicated documents, such as proposed ordinances or statutes, budget messages, and reports of investigatory committees, have little meaning until they are placed within a broader context. Reporters who simply pass on summaries of these documents, without analyzing their significance or suggesting possible implications, serve no real purpose and become, in the words of Pete Hamill, "clerks of fact."

Putting the news in context is not solely the responsibility of the public affairs reporter. Every news writer comes across stories whose meaning would be enhanced by five minutes of research in an encyclopedia or almanac, or by a telephone call to a local authority on the subject. What we are dealing with here is not a writing skill but a habit of mind, a critical stance that enables the writer to get on top of his material and ask the kind of questions that are likely to produce a meaningful story.

The ability to take an isolated news item or press release and fill in the missing information from personal research or telephone interviews is as much of an asset to the contemporary journalist as the ability to write clear and forceful prose. It is a particularly valuable skill for writers on weekly newspapers, where stories that have been superficially covered by the dailies can be adequately researched and given a fresh and more comprehensive presentation.

LOCALIZING THE NEWS

One of the most frequent criticisms directed at newspapers is that they are filled with stories that have little or no relation to the average reader. It is a charge that is not without foundation, as even a brief examination of most dailies will testify.

If we base our judgment on the kind of stories that make up the front page or that command the boldest headlines and the greatest amount of space, we must conclude that the potential to shock, titillate or entertain the reader continues to be a major criterion in determining news values.

The following front-page headline from the *New York Daily News* illustrates this point:

PATTY TELLS
OF SEX
IN CLOSET

If other newspapers were more restrained in headlining the Hearst trial, they nevertheless gave front-page treatment to long wire-service accounts of a proceeding that for all the attendant publicity appeared to have no lasting social significance. It was ironic that Patricia Hearst should have become an unwitting victim of the type of ruthless journalistic sensationalism so successfully practiced by her grandfather, William Randolph Hearst.

It is self-serving of newspapers to rebut this criticism by arguing that this is the kind of news that readers want. This is the kind of news that readers have been getting, with only minor variations, since the 1890s when men like Hearst and Pulitzer discovered that it could be sold like a habit-forming drug to a disoriented and demoralized populace.

In the 1970s, a period characterized by mounting political irrelevance, social disintegration and environmental crisis, sensational news values can be maintained only at great peril to the community. Newspapers that are not actively seeking remedies for problems in their own areas are, in effect, aggravating them by distracting readers from the important work at hand.

To be a constructive force in contemporary affairs, the press must radically alter its view of the reader as an abstract unit of circulation—a mindless spectator to be titillated, entertained and ultimately sold in bulk lots to advertisers. It must recapture the spirit of newspapers during the American Revolution which regarded readers as potential participants in the great events that were shaping their lives.

Bringing this down to the practical level, it means giving high priority to news that is useful to readers, news that permits them to obtain a greater degree of control over their own lives, their own environment and the institutions that purport to serve them. And here the problem is not limited to sensationalism.

The disproportionate amount of newspaper space now devoted to stories about international politics and its practitioners, and the repetitious coverage of national political candidates also cast the reader in the role of spectator and confirm his growing sense of powerlessness. Rather than bombard readers with news of events over which they have little or no control, newspapers should emphasize stories which help the reader to participate in areas where his involvement can make a difference.

To do this effectively, of course, requires intelligent and energetic local reporting. It is always easier—and cheaper—to tear another story from the teletype than to provide competent local coverage, but if serving the reader is a priority there is really no choice. Daily newspapers that have defaulted in this area of public responsibility offer fertile ground for the emergence of vigorous new weeklies.

Another aspect of "localizing" the news that goes hand-in-hand with intelligent local coverage is the effort to make national news more meaningful to the reader by pointing out its practical implications for his town or region. In fact, the degree of relevance of national news to the newspaper's own area ought to be a criterion in judging the value of wire copy.

Even when national news is relevant to the area, the specifics of the relationship must be made clear by local reporters. Often this will require considerable time and effort, but to pass on wire copy that has important local implications without indicating what they are, is another exercise in meaningless journalism.

In the following example, taken from the *Atlanta Constitution,* a "national" story has been "localized" by the newspaper's Washington bureau to give it real meaning for Georgia residents:

> WASHINGTON—A public works and federal aid bill that could mean more than $100 million in new federal money for Georgia and Atlanta passed the U.S. House by an overwhelming 321–80 majority Thursday.
>
> President Gerald Ford announced early in the day that he will veto the $6.3 billion Local Public Works Capital Development and Investment Act of 1975, but the size of the House vote indicates that his veto can be overturned in the lower chamber at least.
>
> The public works measure, passed earlier by the Senate, was strongly supported by both Gov. George Busbee and Atlanta Mayor Maynard Jackson. Busbee lobbied among members of the National Governor's Conference for support for Title III of the bill, which provides 33 states with extra money for construction of sewage treatment facilities.
>
> Title III will bring Georgia an additional $80 million for sewage treatment plants, construction that Busbee said is "vitally needed" for the industrial development of the state.
>
> That section of the bill, also known as the Talmadge-Nunn amendment, was added to the public works bill in the Senate under the leadership of Georgia's two senators. First District Rep. Bo Ginn led the drive for the wastewater treatment funding measure in the house . . .

The story goes on to specify how funds from the bill would be used in Atlanta and other parts of the state and reports on how Georgia Congressmen voted on the bill.

The difference between this story and a wire service account that could appear in any newspaper is obvious. Newspapers without Washington bureaus can add relevant material to the wire story or prepare a separate "sidebar" story on local aspects to run alongside. Weekly newspapers can use all of this material as the basis for a comprehensive feature on the subject.

To stress "localization" of news is not to champion journalistic provincialism. It is simply a way of making news more meaningful by emphasizing its connection to the reader. A strong editorial bias in favor of locally relevant news also acts as a deterrent to the indiscriminate use of wire copy as "filler."

DEVELOPING THE NEWS

Up to this point in the chapter we have been dealing with stories that originate—at least to some extent—from published news accounts. Yet some of the most significant and meaningful articles that can be produced by a journalist are developed from material that has not previously appeared in print.

Writers who wait for stories to "break," that is, force their way into the news by reason of violence, demonstrations, legal charges and the like, are always at the mercy of events. The real story, as we have already noted, lies well below the visible event. But there are many important stories that never become visible at all until brought into public view by an enterprising and imaginative journalist.

What we are talking about here is the kind of story that evolves, not from other news, but from the effort and ingenuity of the writer. The best of these stories often receive Pulitzer Prizes for investigative reporting; all of them offer writers the unique satisfaction that comes from having "made news."

To the reader, "developed" stories appear to have come from nowhere. But the experienced journalist knows that they can come from a variety of sources. Many begin with rumors or tips from sources outside the newspaper. Others may turn up while the writer is researching a story and comes across material that somehow "doesn't add up;" in his attempt to check out the discrepancy, he is likely to find another story. Some of the best developed stories arise simply from a "hunch" or feeling on the part of an alert reporter who senses that something is wrong in a given area or institution, or that there is likely to be some explanation for a peculiar set of circumstances.

Regardless of the original source, the developed story takes its final shape from the painstaking research of the reporter who lets no rumor pass unchecked nor accepts as fact any information that he had not personally verified. Preparing such a story can be a time-consuming and laborious process, and it may take weeks—or even months—before the final pieces fall into place. But a well-written and carefully researched developed story is "news" in the most meaningful sense of the word.

Weekly newspapers that are willing to invest the time and effort required, will find that these stories offer them an opportunity to hold their own against the more routine and superficial coverage of local affairs by the daily press. Many new weeklies have used the developed story to establish a solid journalistic beachhead, even in areas saturated by daily newspapers.

New York's weekly *Village Voice,* a prototype of the new urban weeklies, published an investigative story by Jack Newfield in its Jan. 19, 1976, issue which revealed that Senator Jacob Javits' wife, Marion, was employed by a New York public relations firm at a salary of $67,500 to represent Iranian interests in the United States. Picked up by the wire services and carried by newspapers across the country, the story led to Mrs. Javits' resignation from the position in less than two weeks after it appeared on newsstands.

Not all developed stories are aimed at exposing questionable activities. Boston's weekly *Phoenix* explored the human side of that city's busing controversy in its Sept. 16, 1975, issue by publishing a detailed account of how three separate families were affected by the first week of court-ordered school deseg-regation. The weekly *San Francisco Bay Guardian* has carried at least two in-depth studies of the unemployment situation in that area, with practical suggestions as to where unemployed readers are most likely to find jobs.

Of all forms of journalism, the developed story offers the journalist maximum control over his own material. In preparing the story, he is able to function, not merely as a transmitter of information whose value has been established elsewhere, but as the originator and judge of meaningful news.

9 : THE FEATURE STORY—
NEWS IN DEPTH

Defining a feature story used to be a fairly simple matter. It came down to this: "any story written by a newspaperman that is not news." "News," of course, was the serious stuff—crime, disaster and politics. Features were those entertaining stories about the city's last organ grinder or the dowager who hadn't missed an opening night at the Met since she was sixteen.

As accurate as it once might have been, this definition no longer applies in the contemporary press. Responding to the power of television to involve its viewers in events, daily newspapers have taken the feature story out of the "entertainment" category and placed it squarely in the context of the news.

The transition took place rather abruptly during the 1960s. Under considerable pressure both from television and the strident social awareness of the "underground" press, feature writers turned away from the quaint personality and the offbeat scene to focus on people and issues that were making news. The organ grinder and the dowager were replaced by the civil rights activist, the draft resister and the environmental expert.

After serving for so many decades as a diversion from the news, the feature story now became a device through which news could be given depth, meaning and perspective. In this sense, the feature story had come of age.

The shift in focus of the feature story is apparent in the following two examples, both taken from the Philadelphia *Bulletin*. The first, from 1954, is fairly typical of the period prior to the 1960s:

> Most women prefer a tailored mink stole to a live Indian python to drape around their shoulders, but not Jasmine Goddard of Lambertville, N. J. She'll take the python any day.
>
> Moreover, she'll finish off her costume with a South American boa constrictor wound around her wrist as a bracelet.
>
> The reptiles, however, are only part of her growing menagerie, including a pair of buffaloes . . .

The second, from 1969, indicates that the feature has taken a serious turn:

> Muhammed Kenyatta was helping to organize a black farmers' cooperative in Holmes County, Miss., last April when James Forman called.
>
> "I've known Forman for about five years," said Kenyatta in an interview. "He asked me to come to Detroit for this meeting."
>
> Out of that meeting came the Black Manifesto, with its demands for $500 million in reparations to be paid by the nation's churches to the National Black Economic Development Conference.
>
> Kenyatta, at 25, was one of the youngest persons elected to the 24-member steering committee of the NBEDC at the meeting . . .

What we are seeing is the application of all the traditional feature techniques—plus a few new ones—to the reporting of news. The end product is a three-dimensional story that not only informs the reader, but also provides him with a relevant context in which the facts take on greater impact and meaning. Let us examine some of these techniques.

FEATURE TECHNIQUES

If there is one characteristic that sets off a well-written feature story from other types of news writing, it is that the feature is constructed as an organic whole. Other stories may draw upon specific feature techniques, but it is the feature that goes the farthest in attempting to unify and relate its material.

Thus, a fundamental skill in feature writing is the ability to develop a single unifying theme or "angle" that will provide an organic structure for the material. It is a somewhat more complex task than simply writing a good lead. In inverted pyramid writing, there is a convenient "today" or "yesterday" peg on which to hang a story. In a feature, the lead—whatever form it takes—is derived from the writer's approach to the whole story.

With the following lead, Jack Newfield begins a feature profile of Cesar Chavez in the *Village Voice:*

> Out of the ruin of the 1960s, one remarkable institution and one remarkable leader survived. Martin King, Malcolm X and Robert Kennedy were assassinated. SDS, SNCC and the Beatles fell apart. Rennie Davis discovered a teenage guru. Tim Leary became an informer. Huey Newton beat up an old man and jumped bail. Rap Brown is in prison for armed robbery. *Ramparts* expired. Jimi Hendrix, Janis Joplin, and now Phil Ochs are dead.
>
> But Cesar Chavez and the United Farm Workers endured, and grew, and faltered, and rallied, and became the one tangible thing we could point to and say yes, this is good, this works, this is an example of the world we want to create . . .

In writing this profile, Jack Newfield decided that he would approach the story from this angle: Chavez and his farm workers' union as the only viable movement for change emerging from the 1960s. Around this angle he built a dramatic lead and a compelling story. Newfield might have chosen another angle: Chavez as a combination of radical politics and orthodox religion, or Chavez as America's most untypical union leader. But if he had, he would have written a totally different story.

It is the story angle, therefore, that determines the final shape of the feature and, ultimately, what material will be included or left out. Because it is so crucial to the success of the feature story, the development of an effective angle should be given adequate time and thought.

Some writers refer to this process as "walking around the story." What they mean is that the writer, having reviewed his notes, must now relax to some extent and let the material suggest an approach to him. A good story angle cannot be contrived; it arises naturally from the data gathered on the subject. The writer's role is to open himself to the possibilities inherent in his material.

Occasionally, a story angle will emerge early in the research stage. When this happens, the writer can use it as a guide in his information gathering. But he should not become so enamored of this approach that he is unable to discard it should a stronger and more effective angle turn up later.

Feature Leads

Only when he has developed a story angle that will unify his material around a theme that is both interesting and significant can a writer begin to construct his lead. At this point his objective is to introduce his story angle in such a way that it will immediately capture the attention of the reader.

Since his material lacks the built-in impact of fragmented "hard" news, the feature writer must generate interest by skillful writing. Fortunately, he can draw on a wide variety of techniques—even some normally associated with the craft of fiction. He may choose, like Jack Newfield in the preceding example, to present his theme in the form of a dramatic contrast. He may decide that the most effective lead would be a simple statement of his theme, as in this example from the *New York Post:*

> For Roy Schuster, the 71-year-old man released from state prison recently after 44 years, the little things, almost as much as the big, symbolize the loss of his youth and middle age.

The writer may begin by relating an incident that sheds light on the character of his subject, as in this feature profile from the weekly *Maine Times:*

> Lillian Caron pushed open the door of Victor News and went scrambling among the stacks of sex magazines.
>
> "Here it is," she called out. She reached down to a floor-level shelf to pick up the July issue of *Hustler,* which had a Bicentennial theme. The American flag was displayed as a bikini bottom, only partially covering the woman it adorned. The mayor said in disgust, "How could they do that to our flag. No wonder people don't have any respect for it anymore."

If the subject of the feature is a place rather than a person, the writer can employ a descriptive lead to convey the mood of the story. Here is an example from the *Boston Globe:*

> Dave Chappron dates Debby Daniels. Steve Fischman doesn't have a girlfriend but he has his parents' car. Andy Thorburn is stuck with his homework. And A. J. Manville has his imagination and his admirers.
>
> It is a gray winter afternoon in the peninsula town of Hull. The last school bell has rung and the students are filtering out of the red brick high school near the Coast Guard Station to begin their afternoon rituals. There's time to pass until dinner.

Direct quotes also may be used as feature leads, but they must be selected with some discretion. Beginning writers have a tendency to fall back on a colorful quote as the opening for a feature without first asking whether the quote helps to establish the feature angle. If it does not, the quote should not appear in the lead.

In the following lead to a feature profile, also from the *Boston Globe,* the writer has used a provocative quote from the subject, but it becomes apparent in the second paragraph that the remark cleverly introduces the underlying theme of the story:

> "If my grandchildren called me Granny, I'd clobber them," smiles President Ford's Director of Consumer Affairs, blonde Virginia Knauer, 60, an indomitable grandmother of three who runs her office on a $1.5 million budget.
>
> "They call me Nana," says Mrs. Knauer. She has been criticized by detractors who have openly suggested early re-

tirement from the job she has held seven years, the longest anyone has held the position. Her admirers refer to her affectionately as "a tough old bird" and insist that the granny image is positive.

In some instances, a snatch of dialogue can be used effectively to set the overall tone of the story, as in this lead from the *Philadelphia Inquirer:*

> NEW YORK—"Everyone knew Jimmy Carter had the nomination, so, politically-wise, it was a very boring convention," recalled reporter Jonathan Engle, standing in the courtyard of his Manhattan office.
>
> "Aw, waddya know about it?" put in his colleague, Christopher Clay, as he popped up behind him and squirted him in the face with a garden hose.
>
> Such antics might be frowned upon at the *Washington Post,* but over at Children's Express, a fledgling monthly, the squirting, rib-tickling, arm tugging and pigtail-pulling are taken in stride. After all, what can you expect when your reporters are bright, high-spirited, fun-loving and range in age from 7 to 13?

At this point it should be obvious that there is almost no limit to the kinds of leads that can be used in feature writing. The only criterion is effectiveness. A good lead pulls the reader into the feature by an adroit presentation of the story angle.

Feature Development

The feature writer cannot lose sight of the fact that he is using the medium of the printed word to communicate with readers who are receiving a major portion of their information by television, radio and film. This means that today's newspaper reader has come to expect images as well as ideas.

So pervasive are these expectations that few contemporary newspapers would consider running a feature story without at least one related photograph. But even a strong pictorial display

does not let the writer off the hook. His writing must also contain vivid images that permit the reader to see, hear and touch the subject.

In producing this kind of prose, the writer is not trying to duplicate the work of the new media, much of which, in their respective areas, is unparalleled. His objective should be to provide the reader with images that may be inaccessible to a reporter who must rely on a camera or microphone.

The mere presence of microphones or a video camera can inhibit or alter the normal behavior of subjects, and both the format and economic structure of radio and television limit the extent to which their complex equipment can be employed in a given situation. Print media reporters, by contrast, have almost unrestricted movement and, when necessary, can function as observers within a cloak of invisibility.

Thus, in turning to the feature, newspaper writers ought to exploit the peculiar advantages of their own medium, but they must do so with forceful writing that holds the reader with its texture and imagery.

Feature writing techniques are not a departure from basic news style as outlined in Chapter 5. They are an extension of this style to areas not always open to journalists writing straight news under deadline conditions. In feature writing, the lean prose of the inverted pyramid is applied to the narrative, to description, to anecdotal passages and to a more sophisticated handling of quotation and dialogue.

Since ''order of importance'' gives way in feature writing to a more subtle organic ordering, the role of transitional devices in providing continuity becomes even more critical. Instead of using a transitional word or phrase to change the subject, the feature writer may need a paragraph to shift the scene or relate a topic to the story angle.

A transitional or ''bridge'' paragraph normally is required after a descriptive or quotation lead in a feature to fuse the lead and story angle. A good example is the third paragraph in the preceding story from the *Philadelphia Inquirer*. This paragraph supplies a context for the intriguing dialogue that opens the story and relates it to the overall theme.

In a feature article on Mayor Kevin White, a writer in the *Boston Phoenix* wished to change the subject from increased police protection for the Mayor, to the Mayor's concern with charges of corruption levelled at his administration—a rather abrupt shift. Notice how smoothly the writer makes this change in an effective transitional paragraph:

> There has been police protection at the White residence before, but never, the Mayor said, for a sustained period, and always on the advice of the department, not at his request.
>
> Although the Mayor's fears of physical violence have been assuaged by the police protection for his home and family, he is not any less anxious these days about persistent allegations of corruption within his administration.
>
> In the course of defending himself against the half-dozen or more charges that have surfaced within the past year, White shed new light on one charge that was given short shrift when first publicized last November . . .

The test of a good transition is that it provides a relationship between two different topics. If the writer has taken time to develop a coherent structure for his story, the task of building smooth transitions should not be a difficult one.

One of the techniques that feature writing borrows from fiction—along with its fundamental narrative style—is the use of description to create vivid images. Descriptive writing, however, cannot serve as an excuse to depart from basic news style with its emphasis on brevity and on the key roles of noun and verb in sentence structure. Good description is achieved, not by piling up adjectives in long passages, but by including within the narrative the kind of concrete details that are essential for pungent imagery.

In a *Washington Post* feature about the reopening of Ellis Island as a national monument (referred to previously), the writer offers a description of the historic main hall:

> Walking through the main hall of Ellis Island, a monumental example of Victorian imitation of Renaissance architecture, an eerie silence has replaced the babble of many languages.
>
> The reception room, where 50-foot tiled ceilings arched high over crowds of more than 1,000, is empty. Light blue paint peels off the walls. Plaster lies in chunks on the floor. Huge windows are overgrown with ivy.
>
> The only reminders of the past are the rows and rows of straight-back brown benches where immigrants listened as inspectors called out their numbers in a dozen languages . . .

Here, in a few short sentences, the writer has conjured up a haunting image of physical decay, and yet has done so without using the words. It is the reader who supplies the adjectives. Vivid description does not deal in second-hand images; it supplies the telling detail and lets the reader fashion his own.

Another device that the feature writer has acquired from fiction is the use of direct quotes or dialogue to establish a mood or reveal the character of his subjects. In most news writing, direct quotes are selected for their content, that is, to provide an accurate rendering of an important or striking comment. In feature writing, quotes and dialogue which may contain little or no significant information also may be used if they help the writer to tell his story more vividly.

A *New York Post* feature cited earlier about a 71-year-old man who had been released after 44 years in prison, employs such a quote to emphasize the subject's long isolation from everyday life:

> "Are these roses?" he asked, gesturing at colorful, garden-grown dahlias making up the centerpiece on a dinner table a few days ago.
>
> "I didn't think so, but I wasn't sure. I haven't seen much in the way of flowers for awhile," he said.

The use of dialogue to help set the mood for a story can be seen in the following excerpt from a *Boston Phoenix* feature on the precarious relationship between the police and crowds during anti-busing demonstrations in the city:

> "Anyone who remains in this area," said the MDC commander to his troops, "is a legal trespasser." The order was accompanied by a sweeping gesture that could have indicated "this area" to be anything from "this block" to "this city."
>
> "How can you be a trespasser," a stout, darkhaired mother wanted to know, "when you live here?"
>
> The cop shrugged, a "What can I do?" gesture. "It's (Judge) Garrity," he said, simply.

In both examples, the quoted material offers readers an intimate view of the subject that no descriptive statement by the writer could equal.

One additional feature technique that can provide similar insights into the subject is the inclusion of anecdotal material in the story. Anecdotes are those incidents related by the subject or others that underscore in a personal way, points that the writer wishes to make. Like quotations and dialogue, anecdotes enable the writer to slip offstage and let his characters take over the narrative. When used with discretion, they add vitality and immediacy to writing.

The *Maine Times* used this device effectively in a profile of social activist Alice Bean. To illustrate the subject's own experiences as a welfare recipient, the writer turned to an anecdote:

> Besides worrisome landlords, Bean had to endure "do-gooder caseworkers" when she was on welfare. "God, hon, did I get tired of surplus foods. They kept telling me and my poor friends about different recipes we could use. So one night, I invited my caseworker to dinner to prove to her you just couldn't do much with that crap. I got some dye, and we had green meat, red mashed potatoes, blue string beans. She ate it and thought it was the best Goddamn idea she had ever seen."

Anecdotes are particularly useful in feature profiles where the writer wants to present a balanced picture of a controversial subject. By including quotes and anecdotal material from a variety of sources, the writer sets up, in effect, multiple camera positions from which a complex personality can be viewed in its totality.

Feature Endings

As its name so clearly indicates, the inverted pyramid is a top-heavy structure. When news is written in this form, an inordinate amount of time and effort are devoted to constructing a lead paragraph and developing the major aspects of the story. As the writer presents his least important information, the story dwindles to an end and stops.

Although a stronger ending occasionally may be desirable in inverted pyramid writing, it is not necessary and may even work against one of the major benefits of the form—the ease with which the story can be cut from the bottom.

The feature story, however, is an organic rather than a geometric form. This means that its parts are interrelated and that each has an important function. In a feature, the end is almost as significant as the beginning, since its role is to restate the story angle in a way that will leave a lasting impression on the reader.

Feature endings may be straightforward, ironic or humorous. Like feature leads, they can take the form of a summary, a quotation, an anecdote or a descriptive passage. The essential requirement is that they drive home the theme of the story in a manner that is consistent with the overall tone. A lighthearted or humorous ending obviously would be out of place in a serious feature.

The *Washington Post* feature on Ellis Island cited earlier ends strongly with a quote from Peter Sammartino, a New Jersey educator who was a prime mover in the campaign to restore the historic site:

> "This is going to be the most important tourist attraction in the United States," said Sammartino.

> "I'm not exaggerating. Ellis Island gives you a perspective on America. It makes you realize that, in spite of all the problems we've had, and all the inequities, we're glad our fathers and grandfathers made the decision to come here."

A *Los Angeles Times* profile of Jimmy Carter's younger brother, Billy, approaches its subject in a spirit of gentle humor, noting in the lead that he "ought to be rated 'X' " because of his fondness for beer and whiskey and his infrequent church attendance. The feature ends with an anecdote that effectively reinforces the story angle:

> Back in Plains, when Jimmy Carter was not on hand recently to greet the arriving Sen. Herman E. Talmadge (D-Ga.), his official greeter was Billy Carter, who alighted from the front seat of a Georgia State Patrol car clad in blue jeans and a workshirt.
>
> "Is that the first time," asked a reporter, "you've ever ridden in a patrol car in an official capacity?"
>
> "Well let's put it this way," Billy replied, "It's the first time I haven't had to ride in the back seat."

In bringing a feature to an end, the writer has more freedom to make an emotional or impressionistic statement than in the lead because the reader at this point is prepared to grasp its full meaning. He should keep this fact in mind in selecting material for an ending.

FORMS OF THE FEATURE

Any writing form that is as open to creativity and invention as the feature story resists a neat division into categories. Add to this the contemporary interest in journalistic experimentation, and the task of placing labels on features becomes a downright questionable—if not futile—exercise.

Techniques once reserved for human interest stories now are applied to the news, while skillful investigation and reporting have become a prerequisite for modern feature writing. Reportorial judgment plays an ever-growing role in news and features, and the first-person story—once a newsroom taboo—is seen regularly in dailies as well as weeklies. In short, the old lines that divided news from features and one kind of feature from another—fuzzy at best—have been all but erased by innovation.

The only useful distinction that can be made among features, from the writer's point of view, is one that separates those related to the news from those which are not. Hence, in terms of technique, there are only two general types: news features and human interest features. And even these categories are not mutually exclusive.

This distinction, however imprecise, has a functional value for the writer because it is based on certain characteristics that are common to each category. Let us look now at these two general areas of feature writing. Since the personal profile, whether in the news or human interest area, has several specific requirements of its own, we shall discuss it in a separate section.

The News Feature

The term "news feature" can be applied to almost any feature writing that relates, even indirectly, to a news event. It would include stories that analyze news trends, articles that provide a broader perspective on the news and even descriptive or "color" pieces written in conjunction with straight news stories. It may also be applied to investigative features which, by exposing conditions about which the public was unaware, "make news."

There was a time in newspaper journalism when "feature" was synonymous with "human interest." But from the 1960s on, as feature writers turned their attention to more serious themes, it was the news feature that became dominant. Since the primary objective of the news feature is understanding, rather than entertainment, the feature writer was required to adapt his techniques to this purpose.

A good news feature is a combination of vigorous and imaginative writing coupled with careful research and an underlying concern for factual accuracy. It is a form designed to offer readers a more meaningful context for news; thus, the writer is expected to bring his own informed judgment to bear on the story. This is not editorializing, but the full use by the writer of the privileged position in which his research and observations have placed him.

Because of its unique ability to put events in a wider perspective, the news feature has become the most common story form in weekly newspapers that have emerged in response to electronic journalism. An interpretative feature remains "timely" for a relatively long period, and, in the hands of an experienced and observant reporter, can provide insights and understanding unobtainable in any other medium.

News features vary considerably along a spectrum that ranges from news analysis—in style only a few steps removed from straight reporting—at one end, to descriptive, emotionally-moving accounts of news events, at the other. While the former are built primarily on the writer's critical judgment and analysis and the latter on a strong narrative and sharp imagery, most news features fall somewhere in between and employ elements of both.

A good example of news analysis is the following story from the *Boston Globe* which attempts to explain a new city budget announced the day before:

> The bottom—sometimes fuzzy—line to the city budget announced yesterday by the White administration is a tax increase that could run to $25 or more for Boston this coming year.
>
> This is an estimate few administration officials would sign their names to, but it is an educated guess from what is being said in City Hall about Boston's finances and what Beacon Hill and Washington may or may not do in the next few months.
>
> The $25 figure, which would bring the total rate to about

$222, assumes that the state will pick up half the MBTA deficit, but it does allow for cuts by the Dukakis administration that would reduce aid and reimbursements to Boston by about $20 million.

At the opposite end of the spectrum is the news feature that supplies a human dimension to the news. This one, from the *New York Times,* appeared alongside a front-page lead story on the abduction of 26 children and their school bus driver in a central California town:

> CHOWCHILLA, Calif., July 16—About 50 persons of various religious beliefs gathered at the First Baptist Church early this afternoon to hear the pastor talk about "Christians putting their trust in God to reach down and perform a miracle in our midst."
>
> The Rev. R. S. Van Buskirk also told the very emotional prayer service "to seek mercy for the children and mercy for the abductors."
>
> But others, anxious and fearful that 26 of the local children and a bus driver had been kidnapped, were less charitable.
>
> "I'm all for forming a vigilante committee and getting these people," said a grim-faced resident, declining to give his name, who stood outside the police station about noon . . .

The most comprehensive form of the news feature is, of course, the investigative series. In preparing a series, the writer sets out to explore a topic in the news and to report on his findings, usually in from three to six installments. A series may originate with a directive from an editor to investigate a subject of current interest, or it may arise spontaneously when a reporter seeking information for a single article finds himself in the middle of a much larger story that deserves full series treatment.

Before the Watergate revelations by the *Washington Post* turned a pair of police reporters into national celebrities, most newspapers were reluctant to spend the money required for first-rate investigative features. But the phenomenal success of the *Post* in exposing the crimes of the Nixon administration has spurred publishers across the country to set up reportorial teams devoted exclusively to investigatory journalism. The results of these investigations range from a *Boston Globe* series that disclosed favoritism and inequity in the city's real estate tax assessing system, to a five-part study by the *New York Times* of problems caused by incompetent physicians.

Series writing, while based on extensive research, interviews and possibly even statistical analysis, cannot afford to be dull or technical without losing many potential readers. To make his research come alive, the writer must use all of his feature techniques.

In its investigation of property tax assessments, the *Boston Globe* was dealing with a highly technical subject, but in opening the series the writers led off with two concrete examples of inequitable taxation that any reader could understand:

> Mrs. Ellen Dobbins is seriously considering abandoning her three-decker home on Templeton Street in Dorchester. The $3400 her property grosses a year has gone mainly to pay the $1770 the City of Boston charges her in property taxes.
>
> Across the city in Charlestown, Michael P. Walsh also owns a three-family house on Monument Avenue, and city rent control records indicate he took in $6600 in rents last year. But even though his property made almost twice what Mrs. Dobbins' did, his tax bill was $668.78, a third of what Mrs. Dobbins paid.
>
> In the same neighborhood in Charlestown, the owner of a home that recently sold for $47,000 pays $373 a year in taxes while boarded-up, abandoned houses in Roxbury are assessed at four times as much.
>
> These are but a few examples of the disparities that have been allowed to permeate the Boston property tax system . . .

When the inequities of a taxing system are highlighted in vivid, concrete examples, such as the above, the reader cannot help but be drawn into the story.

Each installment in a series should be treated as a separate article; thus, in breaking his overall topic into segments, the writer must insure that each division can support a fully-developed feature with its own story angle. While there may be variations in style from installment to installment, depending on what aspect of the topic is under consideration, the series as a whole must exhibit a generally consistent tone and strong continuity. To maintain continuity, the writer should include enough information from previous articles to make the current installment understandable to new readers.

The growth of the news feature, in all of its forms, is the most significant development in news writing since the rise of electronic journalism. It is not unreasonable, therefore, to expect that the ability to write good news features will soon be considered a fundamental skill for print media journalists.

The Human Interest Feature

It should not be inferred from the sudden expansion of the news feature that the human interest feature has been rendered obsolete. As long as newspapers exist, there will be a place for stories whose only purpose is to move the reader by their beauty, humor or gentle revelations of the human spirit.

While it is true that the human interest story occupies a less prominent position than it once did in the feature writing area, its role is none the less vital. Now that feature writers have joined general assignment reporters in the pursuit of significant news, there is an even greater need for stories that offer some contrast to the general preoccupation with serious themes.

The well-written human interest feature reminds the reader that individual human beings and small events still have the power to move and teach us by their example. But it takes a perceptive writer to discover these subjects amid the clamor of more powerful voices.

Some human interest features, like the following one from the *Philadelphia Inquirer,* force us to stop for a moment and look with fresh eyes at a commonplace event:

On a clear, cloudless morning, a bit cool for August, the city buried its dead yesterday, between two race tracks and next to a playground.

There were 19 bodies in all, some unknown, all unclaimed, filling odd-numbered graves 501 through 529. (Five were infants. They shared a single grave.)

These were pauper burials—the classic Potter's Field rites . . .

Others single out the offbeat or unusual, as does this story from the *New York Times:*

On the 15 acres of Brighton Beach Baths, a city version of country-club life has been nurtured, where status is won in unusual ways and members often look upon their fenced-in enclave of Coney Island as the Nice of New York.

Some 20 years after this world of sports, card-playing, dancing, eating, social badinage and variants of courtship was supposed to have been replaced by high-rise apartment houses, it is still flourishing, with more than 10,000 members and a $175 fee for a 10-month season.

"Look at these tennis courts," Hyman Cohen, the general manager, said the other day. "If you want to play here you got to be dressed. No bathing suits. Tennis here is for ladies and gentlemen. No playing in bikinis and bathing suits."

Trees, grass and flowers now grow in this land of swimming pools, children's rides, handball and paddle handball courts, picnic and card tables, an infants' enclosure, a miniature golf course, a cafeteria and a dance floor . . .

The most common form of the human interest feature, however, is the personal profile which will be discussed in the next section.

Lacking a news connection as a built-in attention factor, the human interest feature demands a high level of writing skill. To absorb readers in stories of obscure personalities or unusual scenes, the writer must offer fresh insights, vivid imagery, authentic dialogue and language that is free of cliches and stereotypes.

To accomplish this is no easy task. But the writer who can turn out human interest features that make readers pause and reflect—even briefly—on the hidden talent and beauty that surround them, is an asset to any newspaper staff.

Personal Profiles

The personal profile is a feature whose primary purpose is to acquaint the reader with the personality of another individual. If the subject is significant because of his connection with an event, the profile would be a news feature; if his significance stems from qualities perceived by the writer, the profile would be considered a human interest feature.

In either case, the writer is attempting, through the medium of print, to create a three-dimensional portrait of a human being. This portrait will not be a painting, complete in every detail, but a sketch that—regardless of its size—captures the spirit of the subject in a relatively few strokes.

Personal profiles have long been a popular form of the feature. But the power of television to bring viewers into intimate contact with its subjects has put added pressure on print media to approximate this intimacy within the confines of type and photography. For those in newspaper journalism, it is not so much a question of competing with electronic media as it is of introducing to readers significant personalities who are beyond the range of the video camera.

The techniques for creating vivid profiles are essentially the same, whether one is writing in the news or human interest areas. They include the use of descriptive details that help the reader to visualize the subject's physical appearance, direct quotes that reveal the subject's attitudes and speech patterns, and anecdotes that illuminate his character.

From the standpoint of technique, the difference between news and human interest profiles is mainly one of emphasis. When subjects are chosen because of their connection with the news, the reader naturally expects to find this relationship highlighted in the story. Accordingly, the writer gives priority to quotes and background information related to the news event at the expense of physical description and anecdotal material.

Yet, if a news profile is expected to hold the interest of readers conditioned by electronic media, it must contain all of these elements to some degree. Two-dimensional profiles built on quotes and background material no longer are adequate. Readers want to ''see'' the subject and ''hear'' his voice.

To evoke vivid images, descriptive writing is best done in short phrases woven tightly into the narrative, as in this paragraph from a *Boston Globe* news interview with French designer Pierre Cardin:

> Cardin, an intense man with chiseled features who looks like an Abraham Lincoln without whiskers, was born in Venice, Italy, the son of a vineyard farmer. Eventually he became a tailor in the salons of Christian Dior and later opened a small business in the Faubourg St. Honoré—which he still maintains.

A description of the subject's physical environment also enhances the visual dimension of the story. In a *Globe* profile cited earlier of Consumer Affairs Director Virginia Knauer, the writer provided us with a stage setting:

> Today Mrs. Knauer, who has frequent meetings with President Ford, sits in a sumptuous beige-pink office with a brocade-covered couch, end tables and comfortable armchairs that suggest a living room. She says neither the office nor the job is glamorous.

While the Cardin interview is concerned primarily with the designer's views on fashion, the writer nevertheless includes a quote that reveals Cardin the man:

> ''What good is it to be the richest man in the cemetery? I don't eat much—I'd be happy with my bread and wine. I can sleep in only one bed. I prefer to walk through traffic rather than ride in it. There is no exhilaration in power. I am only a man.''

Mrs. Knauer also reveals herself on a quote:

> "A woman who's in a show ring always looks more be-
> lievable in clothes that aren't frilly," says tousel-haired Mrs.
> Knauer. "That's a trick I learned when I had 30 Doberman
> Pinschers. I'd have a fat, wiggly little puppy nestled in my
> arms and convince a prospective buyer that this little animal
> certainly was a future champion. My husband would watch
> my pitch and say, 'Honey, you really ought to be in poli-
> tics'."

If physical description, revelatory quotes and anecdotal material add life to news profiles, they are the essential ingredients
of the human interest sketch, where the writer must justify the
importance of the subject solely on the basis of his writing. Ob-
taining this material in sufficient quantity for a well-developed
story, then, is a prerequisite for profile writing. No matter how
well he can write, a reporter without basic skills in interviewing
will be handicapped when it comes to turning out strong personal features. Thus, a few suggestions are in order about the
conduct of interviews.

It is an axiom that success in interviewing is directly propor-
tional to the reporter's preparation for the interview. This means
that the reporter should attempt to find out as much as possible
about his subject in advance of their meeting. He can consult
newspaper clipping files, biographical references and encyclopedia entries under the topic to be discussed. In the case of
an author, he would do well to familiarize himself with the subject's writings.

When he has completed this research, the reporter should
draw up a list of questions that are likely to elicit significant
comments from the subject. The importance of this list cannot
be overstressed. Without it, the reporter will come away from
the interview with large gaps in his information.

In the interview itself, the reporter must establish rapport
with his subject. Many experienced interviewers begin by talking about subjects unrelated to the key areas of the interview
and bring out their notebooks only when the initial awkwardness

has been overcome. The reporter's manner should be pleasant and not antagonistic, but intelligent questions which indicate that the interviewer has done his homework, coupled with an obvious concern for accuracy, will do most to gain the confidence of the subject.

Finally, the reporter must maintain effective control of the interview. When the subject drifts away to areas that are not relevant to the story, the interviewer must bring him back gently but firmly to the crucial topics. At the same time, the reporter must remain alert for unexpected material of importance and pursue it by further questioning.

The skillful interviewer is an active, creative agent in the interview process—asking questions, taking notes, guiding conversation, but all the while listening for colorful or revealing comments and observing the physical characteristics of the subject.

Among all the forms of the feature—news and human interest—the personal profile continues to dominate. This is not surprising since it offers the reader an intimate glimpse of another human being, and the journalist a showcase for the most sophisticated writing and reporting skills.

10 : THE NEW FORMS OF PRINT JOURNALISM

Television's entrance on the American media scene had all the characteristics of a major earthquake. The phenomenon began with a few mild tremors in the early 1950s and culminated in a series of severe shocks lasting almost two decades. When the dust had settled, gaping fissures could be seen in the area of print media, and the landscape was strewn with the debris of many of the nation's most prestigious publications.

Almost from the time that commercial television broadcasting had reached a significant national level in 1948, its effects on other media can be noted. From the 1950s on, there is a gradual decline in the percentage of the total mass media advertising dollar going to daily newspapers. The decline in general magazine advertising, however, began even sooner and was more accelerated.

Seismographs fluttered throughout the magazine industry on Dec. 14, 1956, when the first shock wave struck the Crowell-Collier magazine group, levelling *Collier's*, with 4 million readers, and its sister publications, the *American* and *Woman's Home Companion*. From then on, there was no mistaking the seriousness of the threat posed by television.

Five years later, *Coronet*, a pocket-sized monthly with a circulation of more than 3 million, shuddered and fell. Then in 1969 came the spectacular collapse of the *Saturday Evening Post*, a magazine that had become a landmark among American periodicals. The *Post*'s end came after the publication had deliberately halved its record circulation of 6.5 million, set in 1960.

Two more publishing disasters were yet to come. *Life*, a

large-format pictorial magazine that had pioneered in pho-
tojournalism, folded in 1972 after reducing its circulation from
8.5 to 5.5 million. In the previous year, *Life*'s major competition in the pictorial field, *Look,* with 6.5 million readers, ceased
publication.

The media tremors set in motion by television broadcasting
rocked the newspaper industry with equal violence. If the collapse of dailies after 1950 had been limited mainly to marginal
and small town publications, the figures by themselves, while
impressive, would have been unspectacular. As it turned out,
however, the television after-shock followed no consistent
course; it levelled the mighty and the marginal alike.

New York City was a case in point. In 1960 the metropolis
could boast that it was served by seven daily newspapers, ranging from the austere *Times,* at one end of the spectrum, to the
sensational *News,* at the other. With the possible exception of
the *Mirror*—a pale imitation of the *News*—four of the five other
dailies each possessed a distinct character and enjoyed a wide
reputation for excellence in at least one area of newspaper activity.

The *Herald-Tribune,* heir to the journalistic legacies of
James Gordon Bennett and Horace Greeley, vied with the *Times*
in international reporting and was a frequent recipient of national awards for its graceful make-up and typography. The
World-Telegram and Sun, flagship of the Scripps-Howard
chain, dominated the afternoon, home-delivery market and had
gained recognition for maintaining a stable of excellent feature
writers.

Of all the full-sized dailies, the *Journal-American* was the
most sensational in tone and flamboyant in makeup. If it kept
alive the Hearst image with strident headlines, pungent writing
and jingoistic editorials, it also provided strong city hall coverage and was a haven for the most popular syndicated columnists
of the day.

The *New York Post,* a direct descendant of the newspaper
founded by Alexander Hamilton in 1800, combined a tabloid

format with a far more restrained editorial style than either the *News* or the *Mirror*. In a century and a half, the *Post* had swung 180 degrees from the conservative views of Hamilton to become an articulate press spokesman for liberal policies and programs.

By 1960, the seven pillars of the Nw York newspaper establishment had taken on an aura of permanence, and only a reckless observer would have raised questions about the future. Yet, by the end of the decade, only the *Times,* the *News* and the *Post* remained on the city's news stands. And there has been recurring speculation among newspapermen since then about the long-range prospects of the *Post*.

Is it any wonder, then, that journalists who witnessed this destruction should harbor a gnawing fear that electronic media were slowly and relentlessly destroying all forms of printed communication? Unfortunately, many writers resigned themselves to a paralyzing cynicism about the future of print media and went on working in a kind of trance, expecting any day to hear the crack of doom.

We have been living with television now for more than a quarter of a century. While the field of print media remains in a state of flux, the broad outlines of the new media situation are clearer now than they were when the collapse of long-established publications dominated the news. From this vantage point in time it would seem that the initial havoc wreaked by television was a result of fundamental shifts in the substrata of media as TV pressure unbalanced existing relationships. Rather than heralding the end of print media, as many feared, the destruction appears to have been a prelude to new and different relationships among media.

It is critically important, therefore, for persons engaged in or planning to enter print media to be aware of these new relationships. To keep alive the expectations of an earlier period or to attempt to revive old forms in a new situation will lead only to further cynicism. Let us look, then, at the new landscape of journalism as it appears after the major tremors of television have subsided.

PRINT MEDIA IN THE TELEVISION ERA

Throughout this book, there have been frequent references to the beneficial effects of television on print media: the new emphasis on "depth" and "interpretation" in news writing, the experiments in journalistic form, the maturing of the feature story, and increased concern with format and graphic display. These, however, have been primarily effects within existing media.

Equally significant is the impact that television broadcasting has had on the structure of print media as a whole. It seems that the TV shock wave, while causing wholesale destruction in some areas of print media, fostered others and brought whole new categories into existence. The best way to describe this phenomenon would be to say that where print is concerned, TV has operated as a decentralizing force. Publications whose success rested on general appeal to a mass audience were struck down, while others directed at a specialized audience have grown and prospered.

Among newspapers, the most spectacular casualties were the metropolitan dailies, many of which had become institutions in their respective areas. We have already called attention to the resurgence in the TV era of the community weekly newspaper and the significant development of new urban and regional weeklies that owe their success to the limitations of electronic journalism.

In the magazine area, all of the giants of general interest publishing are dead. Their places on the roster of successful periodicals now are occupied by magazines that cater to a recognizable segment of American society. Any such list would include *Psychology Today, Ms., Rolling Stone, Women's Day, Seventeen, Sports Illustrated* and *Sunset,* a magazine of Western America. Publications geared to special interests and hobbies, such as *Gourmet, Skin Diver* and *Organic Gardening and Farming,* all have fared exceedingly well in the TV era.

Of particular interest to journalists is the emergence during the past two decades of city magazines in every major metropolitan area of the United States. The best of these publications combine strong graphic appeal with solid investigative reporting on the local scene.

Hence, in charting a course for print journalism in an age dominated by electronic communications, we must conclude that the safest routes appear to be those that complement rather than compete with the role of the video camera and microphone. Let us look more closely, then, at the new forms of journalism that follow this path and the specific demands which they place on writers.

THE NEW WEEKLIES

Of all the forms of print media spawned in the wake of television, the most interesting by far to the prospective journalist are the new urban and regional weekly newspapers. Among the best examples at this writing are New York's *Village Voice,* Boston's *Phoenix* and *Real Paper,* the *San Francisco Bay Guardian,* the *Pacific Sun* of Marin Co., Calif., Denver's *Straight Creek Journal,* the *Maine Times* and the *Piedmont Virginian.*

If all of these newspapers can be categorized as a response to the new media environment created by television, they nevertheless exhibit an unusually high degree of diversity—higher, certainly, than that among the established dailies. Lacking the pressure for standardization that comes from group ownership, national advertising and the wire services, these publications have developed a contemporary style that reflects strong regional characteristics.

At one end of the spectrum is the cosmopolitan *Village Voice,* a prototype of the form founded in 1955. While 10 per cent of the paper's 150,000 circulation is sold outside the New York area—a phenomenon that stems directly from its hard-hitting investigative features and excellent reviews of the arts—the *Voice* considers itself basically a New York publication. And so do New York advertisers who account for 90 per cent of the paper's 700 weekly display advertisements.

At the other extreme is the *Piedmont Virginian,* a weekly with a strong regional orientation circulated in eastern Virginia. Unlike the traditional county-seat publication, the *Virginian* was established in 1971 to provide intensive coverage of local affairs in a "community of interest" that includes sections of several Virginia counties. A conservatively-edited tabloid, the *Virginian* nevertheless has infuriated local politicians by its staunch opposition to real estate development and turnpike construction that would alter the essentially rural character of the area.

Some of the new publications, like Boston's *Phoenix* and *Real Paper,* evolved from the "underground" press of the 1960s. How successfully the two Boston weeklies managed this transition is indicated by the fact that each has a circulation approaching 100,000 that extends well beyond the Cambridge academic community. Both papers' comprehensive coverage of arts and entertainment in the Boston area has pressured the dailies into putting out weekly leisure supplements.

Other newspapers, like the *San Francisco Bay Guardian* and the *Pacific Sun* across the bay, are the brainchildren of former daily newspapermen who envisioned a new role for the weekly newspaper. The *Guardian,* a bright, pugnacious tabloid with a passion for muckraking, has been described by *San Francisco* magazine as "easily the best newspaper in the Bay area." In nearby Marin County, the *Pacific Sun*'s combination of striking contemporary graphics and relevant local features make it one of the country's outstanding suburban weeklies.

Although few American states offer the compact geography required for such a venture, the *Maine Times* has shown that a state-wide weekly newspaper can make a unique contribution to the life of its region. Started from scratch in 1968, the *Times* now can point to an impressive circulation of 20,000 earned largely through its vigorous campaigns against the pollution and exploitation of Maine's natural environment. The *Times'* brand of public interest journalism is packaged in a handsome graphic format and graced with stunning photography.

Few in number and limited in circulation when compared to the established dailies, these newspapers nevertheless constitute a significant new form of journalism. Their true impact in their respective areas cannot be measured by circulation figures nor advertising revenue alone. Most of these publications remain in a subscriber's home for at least a week and may be read during that time by as many as six different persons. But even more important: because of the fundamental concern of the new weeklies with the affairs of a readily-definable community— urban, suburban or regional—they enjoy a credibility and intensity of readership unmatched by the all-encompassing dailies.

If the new weeklies have been nurtured in a media environment created by television, they owe their feasibility, nonetheless, to a parallel revolution in graphic arts technology that has made the starting of a newspaper—once a project for millionaires—an enterprise requiring only a relatively modest capital investment. For all of these reasons, we are likely to witness a gradual flowering of this new form throughout the country as more and more journalists become aware of its unique potential for community service.

CITY AND REGIONAL MAGAZINES

Another new form that offers interesting possibilities to print journalists is the city magazine. A nonexistent category of publishing only two decades ago, the form now is visible in every major metropolitan area of the United States, and regional variations are growing rapidly in number.

Unlike the new newspapers, the city magazines exhibit a somewhat dismaying similarity of format, graphics and content; in some cases it would be difficult to identify the magazine by its design if the front page nameplate were removed. All carry considerable national advertising and are directed primarily to

an upper middle class suburban audience with a taste for gourmet dining, fine whiskey, sleek cars, air travel and expensive
jewelry. Nevertheless, they provide journalists with an accessible market for well-written local features and solidly researched
investigative articles.

Circulations range from around the 50,000 level up to a
peak of 360,000 scaled by the weekly *New York,* a pacesetter in
the field whose wide-ranging articles of national interest lead
many observers to question its city magazine classification. *New
York*'s success in the Eastern megalopolis has spurred its publishers to launch *New West,* a bi-weekly regional magazine
aimed at the Southern California audience.

All of the other city magazines are monthlies. Some appear
to be mainly guides to the good life, offering tips on good res-
taurants, home furnishings and boutique shopping to a privileged readership while generally ignoring the plight of blacks
and other disadvantaged groups at the urban core. Yet others,
like *Philadelphia* and the fledgling *Texas Monthly,* are known
widely for their muckraking and two-fisted investigative reporting. *Philadelphia* took the lead in this area in 1967 when it
revealed that a reporter for a Philadelphia daily newspaper was
shaking down local businessmen with threats of unfavorable
publicity.

The rapid growth of the city magazines and their regional
counterparts, the phenomenal success of specialized publications at the national level, and the emergence of the new newspapers, suggest, at least to this observer, that television, far
from bringing down the curtain on print media, has only set the
stage for a new and even more challenging era of journalism.

INDEX

147

Newspapers (*continued*)
(1910-1975), 2; format changes in, new, 99-100; interpretative role of, 4-5, 100; new formats of, 99-100; Sunday, 24; tabloid, 22-23, 96, 101, 144; and technology, modern, 10, 11, 21-25; weekly, 4, 6, 7, 93-94, 101-03, 115-16, 142, 143-45; zone sections in, 6; *see also* Feature story; News story; News style; Speech story
Newsweek, 4, 23
Nixon Administration, 2, 132

Offset printing, 101
O'Hara, John, 11
O'Neill, Eugene, 11
Organic Gardening and Farming magazine, 142

Pacific Sun, 7, 102, 143, 144
Paragraph, fractured, 47-50, 53
Parallelism in sentence structure, 69-70
Patterson, Joseph Medill, 22
Personal-profile feature story, 135-38
Philadelphia Evening Bulletin, 29, 117
Philadelphia Inquirer, 37, 41, 96, 108, 122, 124, 133
Philadelphia magazine, 146
Phoenix, Boston, 7, 103, 115, 124, 125, 143, 144
Photography, press, 9, 21, 28, 60, 100
Piedmont Virginian, 7, 143, 144
Political Illusion, The (Ellul), 104
Post, New York, 62, 65, 76, 120, 140, 141

Post, Washington, 37, 93, 100, 107, 122, 124, 127, 131, 132
Profile, personal, as feature story, 135-38
Psychology Today magazine, 142
Public Ledger (Philadelphia), 28
Pulitzer, Joseph, 15, 111
Pulitzer Prize, 114

Quinlan, Karen Anne, 65, 77
Quotation marks, placement of, 79, 81
Quotations, 74-90; attribution in, 78, 79, 80-83; direct, 74-82 *passim;* indirect, 78; mechanics of, 78-83; and paraphrasing, 75, 76, 77, 78, 80, 81; partial, 82

Radio, 2, 3, 10, 21, 22, 24, 28, 29, 60, 75, 92, 94, 101, 122, 123
Readability: Flesch formula for measuring, 29; paragraph indentions as aid to, 48; and quotations, 79
Reagan, Ronald, 88
Real Paper, Boston, 7, 143, 144
Reidt, Robert, 19, 20
Revolution, American, 112
Rolling Stone magazine, 25, 142
Rowen, Margaret W., 19

San Francisco Bay Guardian, 102, 116, 143, 144
San Francisco magazine, 144
Sandburg, Carl, 11
Saturday Evening Post, 139
Scripps-Howard chain, 140

PN
4783
.F64